wayne e. oates

the care of troublesome people

people

an alban institute publication

The Publications Program of The Alban Institute is assisted by a grant from Trinity Church, New York.

Library of Congress Catalog Card Number 94-78333
ISBN 1-56699-133-1

To James Hyde, Ph.D.,
my steadfast friend and colleague

CONTENTS

Acknowledgments   vii

Introduction   ix

Chapter 1.   Let's Look to Ourselves   1

Chapter 2.   The Care of the Circumferential
or Back-Biting Person   15

Chapter 3.   The Care of the Authoritarian,
Power-Ridden Person   30

Chapter 4.   The Care of the Competitive Divider
of the Congregation   43

Chapter 5.   The Care of the Clinging Vine
or Dependent Person   55

Chapter 6.   The Care of the Star Performer   64

Epilogue   72

Notes   75

ACKNOWLEDGMENTS

I am indebted first of all to the many people in churches, seminaries, and a medical school who have allowed me to glimpse the pain and suffering underneath the characteristics that make them troublesome to other people, especially in institutional settings. They have taught me much that confirms Harry Stack Sullivan's comment that all human beings are much more distinctly alike than different and William James's comment that we make a great deal of fuss over what little difference there is among people.

I am also indebted to The Alban Institute. Under the direction of Editor-in-Chief Celia Allison Hahn, their people have given me excellent critique and suggestions for making this a better book than I alone could have made it.

I also express my appreciation of and esteem for Becky Timerding, our computer specialist, for her kindness, patience, and expertise in translating and transforming this manuscript—from my long-hand first draft through subsequent revisions to this finished document.

—Wayne E. Oates

INTRODUCTION

Some books about difficult people put all of the burden of the problems on the shoulders of the troublesome people.

Or the "blame reflex" can be transferred from an individual to that person's upbringing or family of origin.

Yes, someone raised by one or two undependable, possibly alcoholic, parents may become a difficult person with whom to work and live. But maybe not.

We must avoid easy explanations for contrary personalities: "He's an adult child of an alcoholic" or "She was a sexually abused child" or any of a dozen or more popular stereotypes of troubled people.

A persistent grandparent may have set a child's life on a smoother track. Or maybe such a nurturing role was played by a neighbor, a Sunday school teacher, or an aunt or uncle. And the public school may have provided role models in teachers and coaches to offset the parental deficiency.

And then, even more mystifying, is what Anthony and Cohler call the "invulnerable child." (Others have used the term the "transcending child.") "When confronted with challenge, the ego does more than retreat or safeguard itself; it attempts to master the stimulus and bend it to its own needs."[1]

I could give the example of a forty-year-old woman I've known for twenty years. When she was very young, her father died. Her mother, who became psychotic, never remarried or had other children. The child was caught up in the mother's illness—a folie a deux—for a while. As she played with other children, the girl began to see that her mother was not "right in the head." When she started school, she quickly attached to teachers and caring people at church.

She has finished college and graduate school with honors. She has been married for nineteen years and is a good companion to her husband and two children. She has published two books and many articles. It indeed seems she bent some potentially devastating circumstances to her own need.

I thank God that the generational cycle of psychosis has been broken in this case. She has never had psychiatric care or a psychotic episode. She has had a long series of mentors who have been caring of her and challenged by her. Their care has been in the line of duty as effective teachers. Her husband is a remarkably caring and wise man and loves her dearly. She also has formed and maintains lasting, durable relationships with a wide circle of friends.

Other people with similar backgrounds would have crumpled under the stress. Each person and situation is unique, with differing support systems and inner and outer resources. Each personally has something, not everything, to do with how he or she "turned out." Each individual carries some responsibility.

This book takes more of a systems approach, which moves out of the "blame frame" into a shared responsibility mode. It distributes the burden throughout the system; no one is to blame but everybody is responsible.

A systems approach says that, within the system, withheld information creates damaging secrets. Whether in the family or in the church, a free flow of information is needed for healthy relationships. When information is held back from one part of the system, conflict arises and troublesome people surface as leaders of subsystems.

Keeping in mind this concern for openness, I have titled this book *The Care of Troublesome People*, rather than *Coping with Troublesome People* or even *Dealing with. . . .* The phrases *coping with* and *dealing with* imply that we are managing or manipulating people.

Troublesome people can become confused when they perceive manipulation, cleverness, or insincerity in someone who is "dealing with" and "coping with" them. You as a pastor may perceive yourself to be cleverly finessing the person. But this leads to confusion on the part of the other person—and yourself. Consider the words of the apostle Paul: "God is not a God of disorder but of peace" (1 Cor. 14:33). The word *care* connotes that these people are made in the image of God and are women and men for whom Christ died.

Let us agree that we will not allow ourselves to see these brothers and sisters merely from a human point of view. We will believe in them when they don't believe in themselves. We will not treat them as "oddballs" any more than we see ourselves as "odd balls."

When we, as pastors and lay leaders, translate system thinking into the pulsating life of the church, we face this question: How can we care for these troublesome people in ways that care for the individual, ourselves, *and* the church itself? We must ferret out ways that integrate biblical and theological wisdom; we must be consistent with our calling as Christians.

In these pages I will focus on five types of troublesome people as they affect the total system of the church and as the church and its pastor and lay leaders affect them. I give special attention to patterns in which these people interact with pastors and lay leaders.

Chapter 1, "Look to Yourself," is directed to the pastor and lay leaders. The chapter includes a self-examination of motives, temptations, and reactions in caring for troublesome parishioners.

Chapter 2 addresses the behavior of people who go around behind the backs of others and say and do hurtful things. This I call circumferential backbiting.

Chapter 3 deals with care of authoritarian, power-driven people who are bent on controlling the course of events by imposing their will and influence on the church and its pastor and lay leaders.

Chapter 4 discusses the care of competitive people who do not keep the "rules" of competition. They compete for self-serving reasons, especially for places of leadership in the life of the church.

Chapter 5 considers the clinging vine, dependent types who overburden the pastor with their desire for him to make many or all of their decisions.

Chapter 6 draws attention to the "star performers" in the church-life drama. They ignore the other players; they are soloists when team work is needed.

For these five types of troublesome people, I have set out to accomplish the following goals:

I will seek a biblical and ethical perspective on each group's characteristic patterns. How can we better understand them?

I will consider some interpersonal, developmental patterns and how they have resulted in particular "troublesomeness."

I will give some clues for empathy so we may care for them as we maintain our integrity and authenticity.

Finally, using a systems approach I will give specific examples of church problems, showing ways the church itself fosters these behavioral problems. This will help church leaders focus their attention on the field of relationships in the covenant of the community of faith.

CHAPTER 1

Let's Look to Ourselves

My friends, if anyone is detected in a transgression, you who have received the Spirit should restore such a one in a spirit of gentleness. Take care that you yourselves are not tempted. (Galatians 6:1)

We are embarking on a journey into the assessment and care of people who are "detected" in faults and transgressions. Here in Galatians 6, the apostle Paul points us to the major hazard of this journey; in seeing and reacting to the faults of our neighbors, we may be somehow tempted.

When we—you and I—speak of caring for troublesome people, we need to look to ourselves. We need to examine ourselves in meditation and prayer before God as we know God in Jesus Christ. For it is this Lord Jesus Christ who asks us: "Why do you see the speck in your neighbor's eye, but do not notice the log in your own eye?" (Matt. 7:3).

James 1:22-25 says,

> But be doers of the word, and not merely hearers who deceive themselves. For if any are hearers of the word and not doers, they are like those who look at themselves in a mirror; for they look at themselves and, on going away, immediately forget what they were like. But those who look into the perfect law, the law of liberty, and persevere, being not hearers who forget but do-ers who act—they will be blessed in their doing.

Soren Kierkegaard interpreted this to mean that the mirror is the Word of God. As readers, we have two options: to inspect the mirror or to see ourselves in the mirror. We can study the mirror (i.e. the Word of God) as an objective record, as absorbingly interesting history, as a dogmatist's power with which to beat others into line, or as an interesting piece of literature. But Kierkegaard insisted that the mirror and the Word of God are for our own self-examination to become a doer and not just a hearer of the word.[1]

Biblical Mirrors for Self-Examination

Several biblical passages provide reflections for looking to ourselves.

Mirror 1: Is Behavior Impulsive or Premeditated?

You and I can step back from the fault of which the offender is guilty and ask, "Has this person acted on impulse or did he premeditate and plan the wrongdoing?" This is a distinction made by criminal law that gets lost in the moralisms of church life.

Some commentators note that the passage quoted at the beginning of this chapter, Galatians 6:1, allows for discussing distinctions between the behavior of a person who does something wrong on a sudden impulse and someone who intentionally plans to do wrong.

Let's consider the example of a person with a long record of exemplary behavior who steals from the church treasury or gets involved in an extramarital affair. This person is very different from the one who has a long record of such behavior. You and I—if we consider ourselves spiritual—are admonished to restore in a spirit of gentleness this person who "slips." This is one of the fruits of the Spirit (Gal. 5:23). We are not to match this person's impulsiveness by blowing our stacks. We could easily be in her situation—facing and not resisting temptation.

If a businessperson in our congregation had to serve a year in prison for an inadvertent felony, would we follow Jesus' admonition—to "visit those in prison" and restore this one to active fellowship in the church? I have seen this happen.

Or would we follow the example of another church with which I'm familiar. This congregation isolated the felon and became one more group that has ostracized him. No process of restoration was in place in this case. Fellowship was withdrawn without feeling or sensitivity.

Might a congregation's harsh response be one factor in pushing someone into habitual criminal activity or suicide? Might it be another contributing factor in a drinking habit or an early death from heart failure?

Restoration often takes gentle and persistent initiative toward a person who is too ashamed to appear in church for worship again.

Even in the case of the persistent offender, Paul encourages us to bear one another's burdens and so "fulfill the law of Christ" (Gal. 6:2). Living in a community of faith calls for "putting up with" the faults of others even as they put up with ours. As Paul says in Romans 15:1-2: "We who are strong ought to put up with the failings of the weak, and not to please ourselves. Each of us must please our neighbor for the good purpose of building up the neighbor."

I recall preaching on this text as a visiting minister in a church's Holy Week series. I titled the sermon "The Church—A Fellowship of Sinners." At the end of the service, I offered an invitation for people to come to the altar if they wanted to join the church. An eighty-one-year-old man came forward to profess his faith in Jesus Christ. He said to me, "I have been attending this church for years. I never thought I was good enough to be a member. But if you are a fellowship of sinners, this is where I belong!" Being gentle, edifying, and patient does not mean that we cannot confront people. If we confront other Christians who have offended us, it is to be in a "spirit of gentleness"—not impulsiveness. Fear lies at the base of much impulsiveness. A person is overtaken by a "spirit of fear." But "God did not give us a spirit of cowardice, but rather a spirit of power and of love and of self-discipline" (2 Tim. 1:7). The mind of Christ is spiritual discipline for us!

Mirror 2: Have the Mind of Christ

> Let the same mind be in you that was in Christ Jesus,
> who, though he was in the form of God,
> > did not regard equality with God
> > as something to be exploited,
> but emptied himself,
> > taking the form of a slave,
> > being born in human likeness.
> And being found in human form,

he humbled himself
and became obedient to the point of death—
even death on a cross.

Therefore God also highly exalted him,
        and gave him the name
        that is above every name,
so that at the name of Jesus
        every knee should bend,
        in heaven and on earth and under the earth,
and every tongue should confess
        that Jesus Christ is Lord,
        to the glory of God the Father. (Phil. 2:5-11)

Here is another biblical mirror for our self-examination: the admonition of Paul that you and I have the mind among ourselves that was in Christ Jesus. This mind or attitude is a self-emptying approach to life and our relationships to other people. This does not mean "doing away" with our own selfhood. Rather, it means refusing to "play God" in people's lives; it means emptying ourselves of the temptation to "lord it over" others (see 1 Pet. 5:1-5).

I see self-emptying in terms of Edmund Husserl's comment, "We do not abandon the thesis we have adopted, we make no change in our conviction . . . we set it [our conviction], as it were, 'out of action'; we 'disconnect it.'" Husserl is suggesting that we suspend our convictions while we listen closely to what our neighbor has to say, while we find our way into her world of ideas, attitudes, and beliefs. For example, we could say, "I need you to explain to me these things that have happened. First of all, I want to understand what these events mean to you. What *you* thought and felt is important to me." We *set aside* our own points of view and learn *first* what the offender's point of view is. (Husserl further calls this a "disciplined naivete" or a sort of mature childlikeness or humility as one sets aside his or her own standpoint and approaches another individual or group with a childlike eagerness to learn from that "other.")[2]

Paul's teachings give the spiritual and theological motivation for this attitude and spiritual outlook. We are motivated if we are doers of the word—not just students of the mirror of God's Word who can give a precise description of the mirror but have not examined ourselves. The work of Edmund Husserl describes a way of setting aside our own pre-conceptions and looking and listening to the fresh revelation God's Word and our parishioners have for us.

Mirror 3: Getting the Other Person to Listen

> If another member of the church sins against you, go and point out the fault when the two of you are alone. If the member listens to you, you have regained that one. (Matt. 18:15)

Another greatly neglected guide to our caring for our troublesome parishioners is Jesus' teaching about how we should treat people who sin against us (see Matt. 18:15-20). Verse 15 (above) is a hard tack to take. A favorite indoor sport of church people is talking negatively and harmfully behind one another's backs. Jesus suggests that we bypass the news bearers and talk face to face with the offender. I have found that this "nips trouble in the bud." Give the person the benefit of the doubt by saying, "I don't know whether this is accurate or not, but is it true that you said or did this?" The news bearer may not have reported accurately or may have misinterpreted the message. Give "the offender" an opportunity to say it in her own words. Then if she has indeed hurt you, you can express your feeling of having been offended. You can give her the opportunity to explain any misunderstanding or misinterpretation or deed. Notice that Jesus' reason for taking this action is to get the person "to listen." It's not to vent our anger, issue threats, or to remove privileges.

There can be another advantage of this face-to-face, private conversation. What a pastor or lay leader does or says is done or said in the context of a powerful system of relationships. Word of your initiating this private conversation might well spread through the church system. If so, it can lift the level of ethical responsibility of the whole congregation. Members will know that they, too, will face you alone if they sin against you. Your dealing with an offender quickly becomes a base of the thinking in the congregational system and its subsystems.

As recorded in Matthew 18, Jesus gives a second step for dealing with a troublemaker: Ask one or two people to join you; see if this small group can get the offender to listen. This step is to be taken only if a one-to-one initiative fails to get someone's ear. By bringing in one or two others, you can check out your own behavior with the wisdom of other Christians. At the same time you have taken a step toward approaching the church with a systemic view. The objective is to get the offender to listen, to "pay attention." It is not for you—or the offender—to "get attention." This injunction is also found in Deuteronomy 19:15, which Jesus quotes when he refers to "the evidence of two or three witnesses." If this small-group confrontation fails, Jesus suggests another step that is most difficult.

Jesus urges that if the offender does not heed two or three people, the offender should come before the church. "If the member refuses to listen even to the church, let such a one be to you as a Gentile and a tax collector" (Matt. 18:17). I am told by many pastors that the bureaucratic and impersonal nature of today's church makes this impossible. The size of the church creates a non-face-to-face system that bears little resemblance to the New Testament church system. But reading church minutes recorded a hundred years ago reveals many instances of church discipline in the sense of admonishing or even excommunication. And denominations with ecclesiastical courts still use judicial procedures for excluding offending members. I have been a consultant in some of these proceedings.

Other highly disciplined communities such as the Amish and some Mennonites still practice "shunning" as a means of punishing an unrepentant offender of the codes of behavior of their fellowship. The hazard of such procedures is that they push the congregation into a new legalism. These three steps suggested by remembered teachings of Jesus must be applied in light of Paul's teaching to consider the impulsive or even compulsive nature of the person's behavior and to restore the person in a spirit of gentleness.

For example, the American Association of Pastoral Counseling has had a recent increase in infractions of their Code of Ethics. Until 1993 the rule was complete dismissal for first offenders. Now the first-offense requirement is a period of probation, during which the person is supervised and is part of a support group. Personal therapy is recommended but not required, because therapy cannot be forced. Restoration is the goal. But if the person persists in breaking the Code of Ethics, showing a pattern of offenses, dismissal is the course.

Returning to our discussion of the church, when a member is excommunicated or ostracized, other members can and should show hospitality and kindness on a personal basis outside the church. The person's behavior may be the result of a severe depression. The suffering is exacerbated if he or she suffers *alone*, outside the fellowship. Jesus suggests that someone who "refuses to listen even to the church . . . be to you as a Gentile and a tax collector." That seems harsh, but Christ's mission in the world at his presentation in the temple shortly after his birth was to be "a light for revelation to the Gentiles" (Luke 2:32), and he took great initiative toward Zacchaeus, the tax collector. Individuals in a congregation can sustain a caring relationship to a person verbally or tacitly ostracized from the church. One hopes that restoration might take place.

General Ethical Permissiveness and Specific Church Discipline

In today's competition among churches for members, Ananias and Sapphira would be perfectly safe. They could have joined another church of the same or a different denomination! Even a pastor who has had an affair with and fathered a child by a parishioner can be discharged by his church, move across the country, and successfully start a new church of his own. It has been done!

The ethical atmosphere of the system of church life today is permeated by a least-common-denominator permissiveness. The covenanted ethic is nonexistent, and when "push comes to shove" in a particular situation, the prevailing pattern is to look the other way or shun the person without any verbal, ethical inquiry as to whether the allegations are true. To avoid being legalistic, we have let ourselves become antinomian or amoral.

A pastor's and lay leader's response to troublesome people cannot be separated from this amorality of the church system. The general ethical permissiveness pervading the life of the church from secular society can be intentionally disciplined by the church. This is not at all easy, however. The real hazard is that legalism becomes a reactionary, mean spirit about the sins of others. Little inward self-searching takes place.

Toward a Patient, Ethical Inquiry

One approach to the need for an ethical covenant in the church is the
establishment of an ethical study group appointed by the congregation.
The group certainly should not be self-appointed! Such a group could
seek consultation from ethicists in the community, draw from literature
on ethics, such as T. B. Maston's *Biblical Ethics: A Guide to the Ethical
Message of the Scriptures*[3] and learn from problems of ethical lapses in
the life of the church in the past. Such a study group would be interested
primarily in developing guiding principles of ethics based on the New
Testament teachings of Jesus and the apostles.

     These principles could be made available to the congregation. The
group could request feedback and promise continued refinement and
clarification.

The Possibility of a Grievance Committee

After a study committee and the church have settled upon a set of ethical
principles guiding members' actions toward one another, an additional
approach could be the establishment of a grievance committee.

     To consider establishing such a group, both the pastor and the lay
leadership must be committed to developing a disciplined congregation.

     Such a congregation would have to be small and intentionally in-
formed, a people who are known to and care lovingly about one another.
A prototype of this kind of church is the Church of the Saviour in
Washington, D.C., which is made up of a number of small congregations.
A congregation as a whole cares for the troublesome person. The pastor
is not the lightning rod for the negative projections and distemper of a
given member. The system as a whole is responsible.

     In a larger congregation, the leadership—pastoral and lay—can
assume that troublesome people will appear. They may already know
some such folk. They might ask for a church-appointed panel of five or
seven edifying members who have the gift of discernment. In the New
Testament, *discernment* means the capacity to make moral judgments of
right and wrong. More than that, discernment refers to the ability to
understand the distinction among the many shades of gray between the
"black and white." We live in a world of ambiguity, and it takes wisdom

and compassion to make these distinctions. The people chosen for this panel need to have such wisdom and compassion (see 1 Cor. 12:10; Heb. 5:11).

From this grievance committee one or two can be designated to go with the pastor or layperson to see if a particular offender will listen. Another New Testament teaching can be implemented. Jesus, in Matthew 5:23-24, says,

> So when you are offering your gift at the altar, if you remember that your brother or sister has something against you, leave your gift there before the altar and go; first be reconciled to your brother or sister, and then come and offer your gift. Come to terms quickly. . .

The committee can insist that the individual with the grievance try to be privately reconciled to the person who has offended her. If this fails, one or two members of the grievance committee who are most impartial and objective can go with the person who has been offended to see the offender. This committee should be a standing committee and not one organized to deal with a particular person after a problem has come up.

The comprehensive principle I am suggesting here calls for the pastor and lay leader to see the church for what, before God, it is—the body of Christ. We are the undershepherds, not the Shepherd. The New Testament teachings of Jesus, remembered by early church members, applied his teachings to the knotty problems of order and discipline. These teachings are not obsolete. They can be used in the day-to-day encounters with troublesome people. I assume that early Christians wrote these teachings down as they cared for unhappy, troublesome people. As they implemented these teachings, they sought the consciousness of the presence of Christ, who said, "Where two or three are gathered in my name, I am there among them" (Matt. 18:20). Forgiveness is the central command, and that not seven times but "seventy times seven" (v. 22).

Contemporary Wisdom

The work of some contemporary thinkers illumines and adds to the wisdom of the scripture. I think of applications to the work of the pastor and the interaction of the pastor with laypeople such as those on a grievance committee.

Isolation, Stress, and Loneliness

Many pastors are tempted to become isolated. They prepare for weddings, funerals, and regular services and take on administrative leadership of a congregation. Then, too, Protestant pastors are usually married and have families for which they are responsible. Then, just when they are not watching, they—we—are blind-sided by some troublesome person. Or we may be so absorbed in settling problems created by troublesome people that we wear out them and ourselves.

We can know that we're not alone. Moses twice got into this jam. "When Moses' father-in-law saw all that he was doing for the people, he said, 'What is this that you are doing for the people? Why do you sit alone, while all the people stand around you from morning until evening?'" Moses told him the people came to inquire of God. When they had a dispute "I decide between one person and another."

His father-in-law, Jethro, told him,

> What you are doing is not good. You will surely wear yourselves out, both you and these people with you. For the task is too heavy for you; you cannot do it alone. . . . Look for able men among all the people, men who fear God, are trustworthy and hate dishonest gain; set such men over them as officers over thousands, hundreds, fifties, and tens. . . . Let them bring every important case to you, but decide every minor case themselves. So it will be easier for you, and they will bear the burden with you. (Exod. 18:14-23)

Another similar story about Moses is found in Numbers 11:15, in which he confessed to God: "I am not able to carry all these people alone, for they are too heavy for me. If this is the way you are going to treat me, put me to death at once—if I have found favor in your sight—

and do not let me see my misery." The Lord God heard Moses' prayer. God told Moses to appoint seventy elders of Israel. God took some of the spirit that was upon Moses and put it upon them (see Num. 11:16-25).

Moses' situation speaks to the condition of many pastors who bear the whole burden of the church alone. They rarely consult with their lay leaders or meet with them, even when the lay leaders request time with them. This creates a leadership vacuum. In systems-theory terms, it breaks the feedback loop. The flow of information, wisdom, and personal strength is interrupted.

The record of Moses' story and the best of systems thinking agree. One can eliminate symptoms of the pastor's isolation, stress, and loneliness by changing the way the church operates. For example, the church might institute a three- or four-person pastoral consultation committee. In one church the pastor regularly confers with the pastoral search committee that recommended her; she does this to "check" on the progress of the pastoral-congregational relationship.

Changing the system works better than attempting to change the symptom or complaint directly. A grievance committee can modify the church structure. The dissatisfied person's complaints are not left for pastors and/or lay leaders to change. Real needs are met. As in Moses' experience, the whole system has been changed.

The Hazard of Scapegoating

A person—pastor, lay leader, or a church member—can easily become a system's scapegoat or "identified patient." This pattern can be seen in the church, the family, or the work place. People come to think that such a person is just trying to get attention. In the church the pastor and/or the lay leadership often obliges this person by paying him too much attention—instead of caring for the larger church system and its families. The individual's whole family system may also be paying too much attention to its scapegoat. He may have been the fall guy for so long that he's taken that identity as a way of life.

When I look at such scapegoating, I see that it should be challenged by the pastor and lay leaders. We need to redistribute responsibility within the system by calling attention to the price the scapegoat is paying. The whole misunderstanding is at this person's expense. Surely the rest of the body of Christ "owes" something to the bad situation. Self-examination calls for each of us to "pay up" and claim personal responsibility for systemic problems.

Pastoral Star Performing and Stress

A part of a pastor's loneliness is the demand upon the pastor to be a "star." In a later chapter I will discuss the troublesome star performer. But to be in character a pastor is often expected to be a star! In some pastors this expectation finds willing slaves. In racing from one dramatic event to another in the church, these pastors become heavily stressed and fail to notice it.

Pastors can become overstressed when they cannot delegate authority and power to others to do some of the work. There are other reasons. Some pastors, carrying a strain of perfectionism, think no one but themselves can do things right. Then such pastors can catch a "virus" of self-pity.

This need for stress-management skills prompts me to suggest seven specific guidelines for pastors:

1. If you have more than one other person on the church staff, have clear, written job descriptions. If your staff is large, have supervisors—in addition to you—to whom staff report on a weekly basis.

2. Be sure that you and your spouse have a cooperative, working, and affectionate relationship and that you "brief" each other in the morning. (What does your schedule look like? What are you anticipating or dreading?) Also "debrief" each other every evening. (How did the day go? Problems? Victories?) This pattern has a way of assuring a couple that all is well with the relationship. If you and your spouse do not have the kind of relationship in which you can do this, consider marital counseling help. Sometimes a conversation with your most trusted and beloved lay leader will provide instruction, humor, and wisdom—instead of or in addition to counseling.

3. Have at least a monthly conversation, or more often if there is a church crisis, with the chair of your official church board. Both of you need to keep track of the pulse of troublesome people—as you maintain a friendship with each other.

4. As I have said before, the stress of being a pastor or a very active

lay leader is never ending. Get away from it all on a regular basis. Some people regularly schedule evenings in which they and their spouses go out for dinner—however inexpensive—someplace where they are not likely to see members of the congregation. Consider a forty-eight-hour "honeymoon renewal"—whether it be at a state park or in a hotel—three or four times a year. This keeps "the home fires burning" as it interrupts the stress at work. Some people prefer taking half of their vacation time in small increments, rather than taking a whole month at once.

5. As much as possible, spread your various stressors out over a period of time. For example, a very tense and difficult official board meeting may be coming up this month. You also face a stressful trip home to your parents' to help them move to a retirement facility. In effect they are breaking up housekeeping. If possible, schedule these two events in two separate weeks.

Multiple stressful events is a primary cause of confusion and even illness, especially upper respiratory ailments such as allergies, bronchitis, chest and throat colds, and pneumonia. Old ailments or complaints, such as back pain, can cause new trouble. Get in touch with your body before it gets in touch with you! (Eat a sensible diet and plan regular exercise.)

6. Build collegial relationships with your lay leaders and professional people outside your church. Making an absorbing friendship with one, two, or three people is unwise, but how can one minister to a couple at their marriage, when their children are born, throughout illnesses, and at the death of their parents, and their agonies of caring for difficult teenage problems without becoming their friend? You are a friend "through thick and thin."

Being steadfast, immovable friends in the work of the Lord begets friendship of the most responsible kind. Collegial relationships with your lay leaders enable all of you to "go through" seamy situations in caring for difficult people. Years down the road, even after you've moved to a new town, you may meet and exchange old "war stories."

Your support system of friends might wisely include other professional people—school teachers, business people, physicians, social workers, psychologists. This group can be a network of informal consultants—warmth and wisdom that encompasses your church. With your church members' permission, you can converse with them about the best way to care for them.

The church is a system made up of family systems near or far. It is also interlocked with a communitywide set of systems—the school system, the law and justice system, the health and medical system, the welfare system, and so forth. Friends in these systems make the pastor more than he or she can be alone. Close friendships can form without creating competitive situations among members. They make the pastor a person of the community and ventilate her life and the life of the church.

This concept of the pastor building a larger system points toward longer pastorates. Such networks are like trees; they take time to grow.

7. Know when to let go of some of the troublesome people for whom you are caring. Most reasonable pastors and laypeople have a natural inclination to wish for close, warm, cooperative relationships with these troublesome people. But some people are by nature detached and panicked by overtures of warmth. They need distance to be comfortable. Your attempts to "help" are perceived as a threat. They may react with suspicion or hostility. Someone once quipped, "I don't know why that person hates me. I never did anything to help him!"

A grievance committee can help give you perspective on when to let go; complaints come to a more objective group after close, one-on-one efforts have failed. Then you are in the position of committing someone to the care of the Holy Spirit and waiting until that person overcomes the spiritual distance between the two of you. In the meantime, you can treat this person as you would any other member. If he becomes ill, you visit him. If she has a son or daughter who graduates from high school or college with high honors, you write a letter of congratulations. You can weep with those who weep, and rejoice with those who rejoice.

If you are rebuffed at any point, you can know you have invaded personal "territory." You can simply say, "Forgive me please for offending you. I just wanted you to know that I care what happens to you, just as I do for all the people in the church." Then you can retreat and pray. Some deep roots underlie such a person's troublesomeness.

Throughout your journey of ministry, you need to take care of your own needs before God and not let the recalcitrant troublesome persons disturb your peace of mind or the life of the church. If you have a fellow pastor nearby, one in whom you have great confidence, get together with that pastor-friend for lunch. I'll wager that he will think that you are talking about someone in his parish.

A few backbiters, for example, are in every crowd—in or out of the church!

The Care of the Circumferential or Back-Biting Person

Psychoanalyst Karen Horney has described the basic source of personal unhappiness in people as the "fundamentally contradictory attitudes [they have] acquired toward other persons."[1]

She describes these contradictory attitudes as "movements" in relation to people: (1) moving toward people; (2) moving against people; and (3) moving away from people. These types of interpersonal movements are critical to the discussion of troublesome people in this book.

I have chosen to add another category of movement: (4) moving around people. People who chronically do this I'd call circumferential personalities or backbiters.

The New Testament, as we shall see, interprets this behavior as blasphemy or sinning "with a high hand," i.e., intentionally and maliciously, against the almighty God. Strong medicine, is it not? A less pejorative approach might say that in moving around behind the backs of others, one sins against the image of God in one's fellow human beings.

In this chapter we will discuss troublesome people who "move around" others; they are circumferential in the way they relate to others. They do not deal face to face with someone about whom they have negative feelings or some real grievance. They will move around that person. They strike with words *behind* that person's back. A message will be delivered by proxy—from some person to whom the backbiter has spoken. It may be a firsthand repetition, but it has often "been through" two, three, or four "hands" before it reaches its target. By this time it is a rumor. Several people have either "joined up" with the critic or become his adversary. In time you as pastor and lay leaders do not have merely an isolated backbiter with a personal grievance. You have to deal with a brush fire within the church system.

Some Patterns of Discernment

Circumferential behavior, then, does not happen in a vacuum but in the church system. The church that does not have a "decent and orderly" process for receiving complaints finds that criticisms come from rumors, gossip, and tattling. It is best to care for these in the local congregation, face to face. But many churches, especially those with a judicial system for processing complaints of individual members and local congregations, can handle such problems in a "decent and orderly" manner. If a church has a denominational judicatory and the congregation comes to an impasse, the judicatory can possibly intervene. Yet in reality, some congregational conflicts are chronic and become a way of life for the people. To say that God in Christ is even considered in such chronic conflicts is absurd.

Pushing personal disputes to this level is essentially a game of power politics. Churches with a congregational polity independent of all other congregations, such as Baptists, Cumberland Presbyterians, and some Pentecostals, usually have no such superstructures. Dissidents must settle complaints locally or let them become church secrets or open grudge wars. People who are uninterested in the conflict or are weary of it—or both—often take the option of leaving the church.

The pastor and lay leaders who do not have their fingers on the pulse of the congregation will get second-, third-, and fourth-hand reports of people who are unhappy. Casual questions such as, "How do you think the church is going today?" will often elicit face-to-face responses that can be useful in shaping the course of the life of the church.

A discerning leader will not see criticism behind every negative comment. Say a person outside the inner circle of leadership says, "At the business meeting last week I noticed that we had lost thirty-nine members and gained five. We can't continue to do that, can we?" This is a reasonable question that does not point the finger at anyone but firmly distributes responsibility to the whole community. Notice the "we" that is used; it is not a "they." It is easy for lay leaders and pastors to write off edifying questions as gossip, foot dragging, and obstructionism when they are not such. They are coming from people in the system who may not have been heard before. If you are at first repelled by their words, remember that "a clock that won't run is right twice a day!" If you see them as opponents, the better part of wisdom is to find what is *right* in their arguments and affirm it and them.

This reasonable approach to criticism calls for face-to-face dealing with the originator of the perceived criticism. When an innocent, helpful question is heard third- or fourth-hand, it has usually turned sour. The apostle Paul's dialogue with the apostle Peter is exemplary. Paul was offended by Peter's shifting stance regarding eating with Gentiles. He says:

> But when Cephas [Peter] came to Antioch, I opposed him to his face, because he stood self-condemned; for until certain people came from James, he used to eat with the Gentiles. But after they came, he drew back and kept himself separate for fear of the circumcision faction. (Gal. 2:11-12)

This issue was put before the whole early Christian church, and the Jerusalem conference agreed upon a policy (see Acts 15:19-21).

Peter's shilly-shallying about eating with Gentiles was but a symptom of a larger issue addressed at this conference. Peter was afraid of the circumcision faction. The conference agreed that the Holy Spirit did not want the church to burden Gentiles with circumcision, but Gentiles should abstain from eating what had been "sacrificed to idols and from blood and from what is strangled and from fornication" (Acts 15:29).

Out of a face-to-face conversation between the two apostles, Peter and Paul, emerged a resolution to a basically wrong principle that would have kept the early church from spreading to the Gentiles. The new policy included us Gentiles. Without this face-to-face encounter one can only speculate as to the outcome.

Paul dealt with Peter face to face; he also did so quickly. He did not let the matter fester and infect while he talked about Peter behind his back, circumferentially. Neither man was a backbiter, though both had the potential. They resisted the temptation. The Lord, it seems to me, will prepare a table before us *in the presence of* our enemies. We will starve if they are absent!

When people in a congregation know that the pastor and/or lay leaders will come to them quickly on a face-to-face basis, they tend to give up some of their back-biting ways. They soon muster the courage to talk face to face.

Perspectives on Backbiting

A Biblical Perspective

Up to this point this discussion has dealt only with the best possible out-come in caring for the circumferential backbiter. But the more trouble-some people may not move with you to a higher resolution of their grievances. The New Testament presents a grim picture of people who are slanderers, a very tough word! In Mark 7:22 Jesus lists slander as one of those evils that comes out of and defiles a person. In Romans 1:28-30 Paul speaks of those whom "God gave up to a debased mind" as " . . . gossips, slanderers." He reiterates this again in Romans 3:8. We sin against the image of God in each other when we do this.

The course of backbiting can careen into the pathology of slander. In the New Testament the original Greek gives an even more stern meaning than the English translation of *slander*. The word in Jesus' and Paul's teaching is *blasphemia* (as in Mark 7:22 and Rom. 1:30). In Timothy and Titus, presumably written for a later stage of the experience of the early church, the word translated as *slanderous* is *diabolos*, speci-fically meaning "devilish, adversarial, or slyly cunning."

This indicates that slanderous backbiting is more than an offense against the covenant of the church. It is a sin done with malice and forethought. But by patiently putting up with the offender, we can, one hopes, work to replace the circumferential communication with face-to-face encounters among the congregation as a whole.

In the case of *blasphemia* and *diabolos*, genuine care can take a confrontational and even adversarial form. Ethical considerations call for these acts to be dealt with forthrightly. Yet the teachings of Jesus and Paul still apply as one confronts people sinning maliciously and with forethought against the covenant of faith, hope, and love in the church. Face-to-face encounter is still a treatment of choice—assuming the issue is not before a secular court. Such an encounter takes courage and self-control. The offender can deny the whole thing, become intimidating, and may walk out of the room. Yet you have done your best if all of this happens.

Perspectives for Preparing a Congregation

The question might be asked: "How do you nurture people so they can become strong enough to stand this tough encounter? The average person cannot."

First, through preaching and teaching *before* a specific case arises, congregations can learn to expect this kind of Christian candor. Not only should they be taught to expect this, but they also need to be encouraged to practice it. This can be kept before a congregation by the pastor preaching on Matthew 18:15-20 periodically as new people come into the church. A sermon titled "Christian Candor," which defines and illustrates both terms, would be appropriate. Adult discussion groups are good forerunners for such instruction.

Second, the encounters themselves can be done in a spirit of gentleness and humility, not with anger and belligerence, by the grievance committee or designated subgroups of that committee. The confronter(s) should have some understanding of and appreciation for the offender's feelings, possibly fear and resistance to a face-to-face encounter with the one(s) he or she has circumferentially criticized. He or she could be encouraged to place more trust in the person circumferentially criticized; you might give assurances that a straightforward suggestion or criticism will be received kindly. The offended party likewise can be encouraged to examine self and consider and even articulate any measure of truth in the criticism. Christian candor works both ways!

Perspectives for Pastoral Ethics

Yet this fearless approach to intimidation also has ethical boundaries for Christian pastors and lay leaders. We pastors can easily become the backbiters ourselves. This is particularly true in pastors' relationships to each other. Such temptation often prompts a pastor to go first to the television and newspapers. For example, in my city a front-page major story reported that four Virginia pastors had charged that a female theological professor had expressed *four* theological heresies in a particular speech. Her school trustees read her manuscript and found all of the charges to be false. Yet damage had already been done by the media. To my knowledge the ministers who started the deception were never admonished, confronted, or even made aware of the damage they had done to this person.

This is a case of pastoral malpractice that occurs often. The media's need for "conflict" to report adds to the behavior's serious nature. Scripture includes an unusual recommendation that ethically sensitive people withdraw from those troublesome people who, according to 1 Timothy 6:4-5, are "wrangling" and have "a morbid craving for controversy and for disputes about words. . . . who are depraved in mind and bereft of the truth."

To me, withdrawing from people who sin with malicious forethought against the New Covenant of the Christian faith is extreme action. Isolation of such people, however, may be the only form of care they will notice.

The Principle of Linkage

We have been dealing with the heavy-duty or slanderous forms of backbiting and the difficulties of confronting such offenders. But seemingly trivial backbiting is much more rampant in congregational life. I say "seemingly trivial" because of what I call the principle of linkage.

For example, a particular issue may *seem* trivial but be *linked* to a larger issue or set of difficulties. This is illustrated by a conflict that arose in a business meeting of a church I pastored. The rural church was considering whether or not they would reschedule services—to "go with" the rest of the state in accepting daylight savings time. This would require farmers to change their schedules in regard to the care of their livestock. Yet this very real concern did not justify the harsh, punitive words that took over the meeting, which ended with no decision made.

Hearing much backbiting from members after the meeting, I interviewed several laypeople. I learned that there was a chronic division in the church, a hidden agenda. The division had resulted in the dismissal of the previous pastor. Some cautioned me "not to touch" the problem; I would "get my ears taken off"!

Even so, I asked for an official board meeting to get the hidden agendas out in the open. The chairman told me that my job was "preaching the gospel," not "meddling in such matters as this."

Refusing to be intimidated, I frankly admonished him that the gospel has much to say about the way people in the church treat one another. The strange outcome was that this "stand" pleased the "silent majority" and won the chairman's respect and even friendship. Considering my predecessor's firing, this blessing was the hand of Providence.

The point of this story is that the undercurrents of backbiting over the daylight savings issue were seemingly trivial. But they were linked to a long-standing church feud.

This is not to say that trivial criticisms do not occur. A person may say to others: "I wish the pastor wouldn't wear the same tie (the advantage of a Christian collar!) every time I see him." If this is what you're hearing from second- or thirdhand parties, try a little humor. Simply change your tie, and when you see the supposed originator of the complaint, say: "I heard from Ms. or Mr. _____ that my old tie was bothering you. It must have been a monotonous thing to see. So I have a different one today. How do you like it?" You may think of a kinder response than this. But in saying something like this you have taken the person seriously. More than that, you will have let this person know that if she talks behind your back about even a trivial thing, she can expect you to face her. (In the end, this may have been the woman's "testing" you as a pastor. Backbiting could continue as a behavioral pattern.)

Creative Linkages

Some of the circumferential backbiting is based in a more creative linkage. Let's say a pastor's family comes in for much third-, fourth-, and fifth-party criticism. A young pastor and his wife have two small children, ages two and four, and the wife does not show up regularly for women's auxiliary meetings. Let's say one of the older women—who has never had any children—asks her husband to complain to the pastor about his wife's absences. The pastor can send a message back to her by her husband: "Tell her that we have two small children. They are our primary responsibility. We have a limited budget, as you know. Even so, baby-sitters are hard to find for morning hours. This comment has called my attention to the needs of several young mothers in the church; all could use baby-sitting help for scheduled, important meetings of the church women. I will talk with your wife, and she and I can work on the baby-sitting needs."

A related issue with the pastor's wife today: She may be working at her own profession. She may be earning more than her pastor husband! For many pastors' wives the time has come when the church can no longer assume that she is an unpaid pastoral assistant.

Two principles of caring for the troublesome person emerge from this example. First, back biters often ask a third person—the husband in this case—to "deliver" their messages, almost like a courier. When this happens, you may ask the same "messenger" to deliver back *your* message. Better yet, go for direct communication.

Second, the critic unwittingly had uncovered a flaw in the system of the church. Women's auxiliary regulars were predominantly older women who had already reared their children or, as in this instance, had no children. Young mothers had not been excluded; they had been ignored. Child care should indeed be available during their meetings. Young mothers should actively be recruited for the auxiliary. Also, the time of the meeting may need to be changed so working mothers can attend.

A pastor might well assess the situation with the leadership of the women's organization. One missing woman—the pastor's wife—and one complaining person revealed in bold relief, for those with eyes to see and ears to hear, a flaw in the system of the church. Some creative ways to change the system would be developed quite easily. The backbiting incident would be used redemptively and everyone involved would be helped by taking this seemingly trivial comment and seeing that it was linked to a larger need.

The Whispering Campaign: Malicious Backbiting

Circumferential or back-biting behavior can become malicious, especially when it involves more than one person. An example? In one church a member started circulating a petition asking for the pastor's resignation. Knowledge of this came to the pastor's attention when a person friendly to him and to the petitioner told the pastor of the petition without naming the petitioner. The lay leadership of the church ferreted out the person and confronted him about the wrongfulness of the action. It was actually a part of a larger "whispering campaign" to get rid of the pastor. A large proportion of the church membership knew nothing of this, but a considerable number were actively promoting the resignation of the pastor.

Whispering campaigns can be a vicious breach of the covenant that binds a church together. The work of one person can debilitate the life of the church as a whole. Sometimes such campaigns are symptoms of a vacuum in the leadership of the whole system. A pastor may have been so battered by other forms of rejection that she has withdrawn from administrative tasks to the public and pastoral functions of the work of ministry. Lay leaders may not even have noticed this withdrawal and subsequent vacuum of leadership. A "petition circulator" can be sucked into this systemic power vacuum and begin a behind-the-scenes campaign to get rid of the pastor. One would hope that the petitioner would relinquish his or her self-appointed powers. But to plan on such a change of heart and mind—and tactic—can be a land mine for the pastor.

Whispering campaigns often involve a deliberately circulated rumor. To the pastor and lay leadership a rumor is an intensely important concern and data—made intense by the lack of concrete evidence to substantiate it. As the rumor spreads, the vacuum of information is filled in with assumptions made by each hearer and repeater. By the time the rumor reaches the person it is about, the content may be a grotesque representation.

Rumor distribution is a standard part of psychological warfare. In time of war, such as World War II, the strategy is purposely used to confuse the enemy. Just after World War II, Gordon Allport, professor of psychology at Harvard, wrote a book, based on wartime experiences, titled *The Psychology of Rumor.* [2] He said the key to stopping a rumor is to inject accurate information where the information at hand is highly vague, ambiguous, and confusing. Rumor is effectively used in political campaigns. No one takes credit for starting the malicious rumors. The damage to the opponent is done.

When this essentially secular tool is used in the church to gain an individual or subgroup's goals and power, the whispering campaign tragically violates the covenant of truth, love, and ethical responsibility of the community of faith.

The Misuse of Parliamentary Procedures

Circumferential, back-biting behavior can appear when someone misuses the parliamentary procedure. I cite several examples of this.

A pulpit search committee "unanimously" recommended a pastoral candidate. Actually, the vote had been about a two-thirds majority. But the committee decided to "make" it unanimous. The dissenters "went along to get along." But their opposition continued after the pastor had taken office. Less than three weeks after the pastor came to the church, a person made a motion in the official board meeting that the pastor be asked for his resignation. Both portions of this tragedy—before and after the pastor arrived—represent a serious misuse of parliamentary procedures. Neither time was the pastor addressed honestly or face to face. Once hired, he was embarrassed by the out-of-the-blue parliamentary motion made at an official board meeting. It was a shot in the back.

The "motion died for a lack of a second." But the motion maker was never held responsible for his misdemeanor. The damage had been done. The chairperson could have appointed someone to meet with this man and the pastor to discuss the opposition and to nail down what prompted the "motion." As it was, the matter was ignored, left to fester and infect the whole system of the church. I imagine many church members were probably telephoning one another after that meeting to discuss what had happened.

Similar misuses of the parliamentary process are seen at the denominational level. In regional and national conventions, matters will be raised in "resolutions" presented on the floor. In a recent convention of the Southern Baptists, a resolution was introduced to censure the president of the United States for his positions on abortion and homosexuality. Similar resolutions were introduced to admonish his local church in Little Rock, Arkansas, for not controlling his political positions. There seems to be no evidence of previous private, face-to-face conversation or correspondence with the president as a member of the church or with the pastor in Little Rock. Several months after the convention representatives finally talked with Clinton personally. President Clinton's home pastor arranged a recent meeting with conservative Southern Baptist representatives. The president is quoted as saying:

> If people of faith treat issues about which they disagree as nothing more than a cause for a screaming match, then we also trivialize religion in our country and we undermine the ability to approach one another with respect and trust and faith.[3]

Christians "screaming" in the media seems to have become the rule rather than the exception. Such behavior is rooted in the desire for publicity.

The teachings of Jesus in Matthew 18:15-20 return to haunt us in both the parliamentary and the media-driven use of backbiting. The contemporary "business meeting" of a local church is generally built on the model of the colonial town hall meeting. The New Testament teachings outlining a specific procedure for handling back-biting violations of the covenant do not appear anywhere in town-meeting "rules" or "codes." It seems to me that pastors and lay leaders would do well to incorporate these teachings into their polity. For example, when a "resolution" attacking a person is introduced, it might be standard procedure to require that the two parties first talk alone about the disagreement. If this fails, they would be required to take one or two other members with them to work toward reconciliation. Only then would a resolution be *in order*. In short, any such resolution would be out of order until the first two steps in Matthew 18 were fulfilled. (Note that the second of these steps —taking one or two "witnesses" to establish whether or not the offender refuses to listen—is older by far than Jesus' teaching. It is found in Deuteronomy 19:15.)

It is possible to *care* for the circumferential backbiter in stern, not just sentimental, ways. The most effective time to introduce these procedures into the church's rules of order is when no particular problem is brewing. This way it becomes a teaching ministry for any who are unaware of the Gospel passage and a warning to any who would seek to hurt others maliciously in an open business meeting of the church.

Some Common Responses of Pastor and Lay Leaders

Without these suggested patterns of discipline, pastors and lay leaders are thrust back on their own resources to care for the backbiter as they care for themselves. Several responses are commonplace:

Becoming Depressed

Some pastors are deeply crushed by back-biting, anonymous letters, and malicious treatment. They become depressed, withdrawing to their preaching and pastoral duties, trying to ignore the slander or *blasphemia*. They lose their initiative and are immobilized. In discouragement they often begin looking for a more hospitable place to work.

If the pastor decides to stay and not move to a new congregation, wisdom calls her to face the depression and deal with it. First, by consulting the family physician. A second step is to seek out a colleague certified in pastoral counseling; explore the roots of the depression in old schemas or tapes established in one's formative years.

In short, deal with the depression, develop initiative, and in a forthright manner confront back-biting church members instead of being bogged down in despair with their tactics.

Becoming Manipulative

Manipulation is another way of relating to backbiters. An example would be "calling out the palace guard." Many pastors maintain control of their positions by ingratiating themselves to a ring of power figures in the church. These people tend to "call the shots" in church management. The pastor who is a manipulator confides in this guard his problems with troublesome people. He expects them to take care of sticky situations for him. In these instances the backbiters often leave the church. This seems to work until so many people leave and finances fall so sharply that the pastor loses his most-favored-person standing in the guard's line-up.

Becoming a "Wisdom Seeker"

A less cynical approach is for a pastor to search the congregation for people of wisdom such as the psalmist described:

> O Lord, who shall sojourn in your tent?
> Who may dwell on your holy hill?
> Those who walk blamelessly, and do what is right,
> and speak the truth from their heart;
> who do not slander with their tongue,
> and do no evil to their friends,
> nor take up a reproach against their neighbors; . . .
> who stand by their oath even to their hurt. (Ps. 15:1-4)

In each community such people are quietly present. They may or may not be members of your church. Seek them out and ask their wisdom. Often they are aware of the history of a particular congregation and its troublesome people from long years of living there. They will provide a wider view of the whole community system. When I have sought out such people, I have come away feeling that I have partaken of the presence of God. I have taken on a calmer and steadier perception of life and can put the words of slanderers in a mode of understanding and even forgiveness that was out of my reach before our conversation.

After such conversations I am ready to care, on a face-to-face basis, for the backbiter—fearlessly and with a serenity that only God can give. We can leave the results in God's hands and remove the offender from the center of our attention. He or she is no longer obscuring God's place in our lives.

Engaging an Outside Consultant

And yet the conflict in the church may continue to rage. Neither pastors nor lay leaders are pleased by the stalemate. The best efforts of people of goodwill are stymied. At this point if all parties agree to do so, an outside consultant-mediator might be asked to work with the church toward a resolution of the conflict. Such stubborn conflicts often represent power-play activity. If the power can be redistributed under the guidance of an outside consultant-catalyst, all can breathe more easily and each can "save face." The great tragedy occurs when a church takes on such conflict as a way of life and lets it rage for decades.

This need not be. You can inform yourself about managing conflict by reading excellent literature on conflict resolution approaches.[4]

If you wish to use the services of an outside consultant, The Alban Institute has five senior consultants on their staff and a network of 35 other consultants in conflict management all over the country.[5] One may be near you. Then, again, you may have in your own community professionals not involved in your church's problems who are people of wisdom and maturity. They are trusted and respected by all parties as "having no axe to grind." Regional denominational offices are increasingly adding conflict management specialists to their staffs.

What If the Backbiter Is Telling the Truth?

What might appear as circumferential, back-biting behavior may, in some cases, be the sincere alarm of parishioners who have solid evidence that demonstrate actual wrong-doing on the part of the pastor or lay leader. They may have talked face-to-face with the offender. He or she rebuffed them, denied the accusation in the face of incontrovertible evidence, and "stone-walled" the whole thing.

The two most frequent behaviors in this category are mismanagement of church funds and sexual misbehavior. Today, evidence of sexual misconduct is far more frequent than the mismanagement of funds.

The purpose of this book is not to explore sexual misconduct of ministers and lay leaders. But when these instances are more than simply "alleged" events, the first response of many congregants is to ignore the information, to consider it as vicious gossip and backbiting. They then act as if nothing is happening by shoving the matter "under the rug." People who have entrusted deep confidence in a pastor or lay leader are reluctant to have their hero revealed as a sex offender. Then, too, if the church has just raised pledges for several million dollars for a new building, such behavior of the pastor is a financial calamity.

Once again, I say this is not a book about sexual misconduct. Excellent books are available that cover that subject comprehensively.[6]

Church judicatories—such as directors of missions or district superintendents among free church traditions, diocesan overseers, and Catholic bishops—and even Pope John Paul II are "aware of the serious nature of the scandal caused by priest sex abuse" and are establishing ways of preventing, confronting, and treating the situations where it is happening.[7]

Such issues facing modern church leaders make pastors and lay leaders cringe. Don't cringe. The world is full of stuff like this. There is no place to run. Stand still and calm your anxiety. Maintain a sense of humor because much of caring for the troublesome people in the church is so serious that it can become ridiculous!

CHAPTER 3

The Care of the Authoritarian, Power-Ridden Person

The leading layperson in a church of seven hundred resident members was also the church's major financial donor. Throughout the church community and the small town, conventional wisdom agreed that this man "called the shots" and "ruled the roost"; he was derisively called "the ramrod."

For the first three years of a pastor's tenure at this church, he and this particular layman got along quite well. Things turned sour, however, when the pastor initiated a building plan without consulting this authoritarian, power-ridden layman. He immediately opposed the building program. A power struggle between this layman and the pastor became the talk of the town as well as the church.

The power struggle came to a head when the layman stood up in a regular business meeting and made a motion that the pastor be asked for his resignation; if the pastor stayed on, he—the layman—would leave the church and join another congregation. (This was a Baptist church; the vote of the congregation was final and not subject to review or reversal by a higher ecclesiastical authority.)

In this case one wonders what prompted the pastor to recommend something as large as a building program without advising the layman. Such a decision calls for a consensus of the whole congregation, especially in a free-church or Baptist tradition. One also wonders why this parishioner was not informed? To leave such an authoritarian, power-ridden person out of the consensus building seems to reflect, to say the least, a pastor's passive-aggressive tendency.

A French proverb seems to apply to this pastor: "For the response, you are responsible." In American slang, the pastor was "asking for it" when he excluded the man from the decision-making process. One must examine the whole set of relationships in the church to have an overall grasp of the situation. Were there other people resisting the building program? Did this man have a following, and was he speaking for this following? Who were the laypeople pushing for a building program? Or was this something the pastor himself was pushing without a consensus? It is possible that the pastor and the layman were expressing equal degrees of rage, one passively and the other aggressively and hostilely?

A Profile of the Authoritarian, Power-Ridden Person

Intimidation

The authoritarian, power-ridden person relies on intimidation, not friendly persuasion, to get his or her way. Intimidation is the act of threatening a person or people so as to make them afraid. Literally, intimidation aims to make the other person timid. He or she is frightened or supposed to be frightened by the intimidator who expects to be obeyed immediately. The man who asked for the pastor's resignation expected his motion to be enacted "on the spot."

A large congregation ordinarily has a constitution, by-laws, and rules of order. In such a case, a motion by any person to discharge a member of the staff cannot be carried out immediately. The motion ordinarily would be referred to the personnel committee for careful deliberation. Even with this kind of organizational resource, the pastor would be wise to go to the man who asked for his resignation and talk with him privately. In a committee meeting, the pastor should be asked why he had not, if indeed he had not, chosen to confer personally with the angry church member. Here also the power-driven person would have an orderly opportunity to state his complaints about the pastor. If the committee is wise, it will ask the pastor and the angry church member to set a time when they will talk privately about their differences, reminding them of the scriptural commands in Matthew 18:15-20. If they do so and if they cannot get each other "to listen," a second meeting with one or two mediators should be held to see if the two can be reconciled. Then and only then would the committee report back to the church with any kind of recommendation concerning the tenure of the pastor.

Such a process gives the pastor and his opponent an opportunity to become more authentic with each other. As Michael and Deborah Bradshaw Jinkins insist, the congregation must perceive the pastor to be spiritually and personally authentic. In turn, the pastor must perceive as

> genuine the religious values and directedness of the congregation, and unless a people perceives as genuine the religious life of their minister, the two will remain fundamentally at odds. When, however, they share a sense of religious authenticity, . . . a positive consensus-base can be effected.[1]

In addition to this, John C. Harris points out that the "structural de pendence" of the pastor puts a "special, though often unconscious, pressure upon the clergy." By "structural dependence" he means that the pastor depends upon the congregation or the denominational hierarchy for economic support. More than this, the pastor gets personal, vocational identity from being a pastor. Few pastors have an alternative way of making a living, and their self-concepts are wrapped up in being clergy.[2] Having a leading lay person publicly demand a pastor's resignation can throw the pastor into total insecurity. Resisting intimidation is a major demand and source of stress, especially when the intimidator has much money, power, and influence.

The Authoritarian's Use of Money as Power

In the lead anecdote of this chapter, the lay leader was not only steering the direction of the church, but he was also a main source of its financial support. Money talks in a power struggle. The pastor was asking the church to start a building program. This called for a major outlay of money. The church was caught in the dilemma of losing either the pastor or a layman with a significant source of money. The pastor had, intentionally or not, put the congregation in a severe bind. This itself might well reduce the congregation's perception of the genuineness of the pastor. How he responds to the threat of the authoritarian, power-ridden man's challenge will either increase or decrease the perceived authenticity of the pastor.

Few pastors have an alternative way of earning a living. The apostle

Paul and Priscilla and Aquila all had the same trade of making tents (see Acts 18:3). They were not dependent upon congregations for a living. Today pastors entering the ministry after having succeeded in a trade or a profession are more secure than those who have no other ready means of livelihood. Remarkably, many older people are now entering seminaries. In one sample of eighty students, I found one out of five to be older than thirty-five and adept at making a living at some trade or profession other than the ministry. Many seminaries have a higher percentage than this. A noticeably large number of people entering the ministry have taken early retirement from other professions and have the security of a pension. Military officers—both line officers and chaplains—have pensions after twenty or thirty years of service. Such people are more experienced and more mature than the student who enters seminary having graduated from college the previous spring. They can maintain their credibility more readily than can a young, inexperienced pastor whose sole income is from the church.

A young pastor would be well advised to learn an alternative way of earning a living. Becoming certified in the American Association of Pastoral Counselors and/or the American Association of Marriage and Family Therapists gives one professional credentials and professional options compatible with being a pastor. Becoming experienced and trained as a conflict resolution consultant is another alternative. Or a pastor might have a hobby such as furniture making that can be turned into some financial support. During the Great Depression I saw much of this. One pastor put his children through college by keeping bees! The bees worked for him while he carried out his pastoral duties. He sold his honey on the road, between stops to visit the sick and the homebound.

Caring for the Authoritarian One on One

If the congregation does not have an appropriate committee to arbitrate this conflict, you, as a pastor, can appeal to the scriptural teachings in Matthew 18:15-20. You can seek a private face-to-face conference with the authoritarian, power-ridden person. His usual complaint is that you did not confer with him. This was indeed a mistake. You can admit to him that you made this mistake. He may have been on a long vacation in Florida while the decision was in the making. If so, you could have called him long distance. Or you could have written him. At any rate, he had been left out; it was a mistake. You can ask his forgiveness. This meeting should be just the two of you. Power-ridden people tend to need an audience to effect their power moves. They are rarely as difficult when the encounter is one on one. Meeting the authoritarian privately lets her know that the pastor is not afraid of her and enables her to follow Jesus' teachings in Matthew 5:23-26:

> So when you are offering your gift at the altar, if you remember that your brother or sister has something against you, leave your gift there before the altar and go; first be reconciled to your brother or sister, and then come and offer your gift. Come to terms quickly with your accuser while you are on your way to court with him, or your accuser may hand you over to the judge, and the judge to the guard, and you will be thrown into prison. Truly I tell you, you will never get out until you have paid the last penny.

This takes "nerve" or *chutzpa*, but it delivers a much needed message to the authoritarian, power-ridden person: You are not afraid of her. You have not received a spirit of timidity but of "power and of love and of self-discipline" (2 Tim. 1:7).

The main objective of this first step toward reconciliation is to get the person "to listen," to hear you out. The pastor in our vignette can tell the layman that he made a mistake in not including him in the planning of a building program. He can ask his forgiveness for this offense against him. If you were this pastor, you could say that your main interest is not whether the building plan goes ahead or whether you keep your job as pastor; your main concern is your care for his spiritual well-being as a person made in the image of God and for whom Christ died. You do not want to lose him as a friend. If he does listen, "you have gained your brother," as Jesus the Christ says.

If he does not listen and refuses to forgive and be reconciled, you can ask one or two persons of wisdom and patience to meet with you and him. Repeat your quest for his understanding, forgiveness, and listening. If he does listen, you have gained your brother (or sister). If he or she does not hear you, you can take a third step, a modern version of Jesus' third approach toward reconciliation. At a called business meeting of the church, you can ask that all efforts for a building program be tabled until a wholehearted consensus is reached. It would be unwise to embark on such an important step until you have a consensus. Then you can confess to the whole church that you had wronged the authoritarian, power-ridden person, had sought his forgiveness in private, then had done so with the two witnesses without results. You want the church in business session to know this and to correct your mistake by deferring the efforts for a building program until a consensus, including the offended member, has been reached either to drop the whole plan or move ahead with the whole church behind the plan. If the autocrat is present, he could be asked to present his points to the whole church. You can ask the church to present their ideas and suggestions at this point.

The need for the autocrat to "save face" is a powerful force, and your admission of fault helps him save face. Your own authenticity is established as well. Power-ridden people are bullies of anyone they sense is afraid of them. The calm fearlessness that God gives you enables you to care honestly, gently, and with self-control for this authoritarian person. It does nothing but harm to the impulsive autocrat to humiliate him or her in the community of faith.

A Systems View of the Authoritarian, Power-Ridden Person

Closer attention is needed from another angle of vision. Let us look again at the problems presented by the authoritarian, power-ridden person. Being so visible in the system, it is easy for this person to become a congregational scapegoat for all the difficulties in the community of faith. A close inspection reveals a system in which this person is blamed for everything that goes wrong. Yet the autocrat may be only the tip of the iceberg in terms of an unhealthy system. For example, this person may have rescued the church in times of financial shortages. Instead of distributing responsibility for this shortage over all the membership, the leadership may sit passively waiting for her to dash in and be the hero who rescues them all. At a deep level they resent this person because they have let themselves be dependent upon her.

Back to our opening vignette, this man probably has family members in the church who have married into other church families. If the issue of the pastor's resignation came to a vote, they would tend to vote against the pastor and with their family patriarch.

The system becomes more involved if we posit that this man is an employer in the main business or factory in the town; many of his employees are members in the church. They would probably vote with their employer and against the pastor. The pastor is "here today and gone tomorrow," but their employer is here to stay. They have to live with him, not with the pastor.

Remember that the pastor is essentially an outsider to this semi-incestuous system. His adversary is a powerful "insider" force. As an outsider, the pastor is expendable.

The longer a pastor has served at the church, the less likely she is to be an outsider. A long-tenured pastor has performed the weddings of many couples, conducted the funerals of their parents, baptized their children, stood with some of them when they became unemployed or went into bankruptcy. Such a pastor has earned what E. P. Hollander calls "idiosyncratic credit." He says, "This represents an accumulation of positively disposed impressions residing in the perception of relevant others."[3]

Think in terms of a pastor having a bank account in which influence or credit (as in *recognition*) is deposited. When the pastor earns credit, it is deposited to his or her "influence account." When change is needed in the church, he or she draws out some of these deposits of influence. A pastor who has not been in a place long enough to have built up an "account" of influence needs to go very slowly about making changes, such as a building program. Efforts should be made to build a consensus before any changes are undertaken. This adds to the influence of a pastor.

On the negative side of the issue of influence, John C. Harris says the autonomy and authenticity of a pastor diminish when the pastor lets personal anxiety undermine his or her leadership. Harris describes a situation in which a hospitalized man asked his pastor for communion. The pastor agreed and went to his car to get the communion materials. Within earshot of the man's room, the pastor met the man's wife. She forbade him to give communion, saying that her husband was an alcoholic. He returned to the man's room and told him that he did not have any bread and would return the next day. The man confronted the pastor and told him that he had overheard the hallway conversation. The man told the pastor to leave; he had caught him in a lie. The pastor's anxiety had caused him to lose all freedom and authenticity in the man's eyes.[4] Chances are high that such a story would become common knowledge in the congregation, further undermining the pastor's autonomy and authenticity. He had recklessly spent much of his idiosyncratic credit.

The Authoritarian Personality

Let's take a closer look at characteristics of the authoritarian personality, which has been thoroughly studied by T. W. Adorno and his associates. Although it is an old study, its substance is still valid. The study includes three characteristics of an authoritarian personality.[5]

First, such people repress all feelings of weakness in themselves and tend to hold all signs of weakness with contempt or lack of feeling altogether. Toughness and "manliness" are premium values. An authoritarian woman will think a kind man is a "wimp." Tenderness and sympathy are viewed as signs of weakness. I have recommended that a pastor who has made mistakes admit the mistakes to the authoritarian parishioner. This can be interpreted as a weakness. But when a pastor admits a mistake in the presence of one or two other witnesses, and/or in a whole business meeting in the authoritarian person's presence, it will be evident that admitting a mistake is not a weakness but a strength. The authoritarian person has mistaken a real strength for a weakness. He or she has been revealed as a tyrant.

Second, the authoritarian person usually has a "palace guard" of people who depend on him or her for leadership. In a church, this group becomes a clique or a power group moving at their leader's command. Evidenced in "voting as a block," this is very common in secular and ecclesiastical politics.

A clique can carry on a persistent harassment of a pastor in a clandestine way obscured from the larger majority of the church which is shocked and angered when the pastor actually resigns. The pastor's leaving brings the whole hidden agenda out in the open and reveals a split congregation. While the church is without a permanent pastor, the leadership does well to seek an outside conflict-resolution consultant to mediate the cleavages. An interim pastor might serve this function in the congregation. A denominational office may have a conflict consultant on staff. Or some highly respected and carefully chosen retired pastors may serve as conflict consultants.

Third, the authoritarian personality generally needs to have a person to *sacrifice*. This need for a sacrificial offering lies deep within the psyche of such people and/or their clique. The demand for the resignation of someone makes that person a totem of sorts. Take the example of the apostle Paul in prison, as recorded in Acts 23:12-13. Paul's nephew notified Paul's captors that the "Jews joined in a conspiracy and bound themselves by an oath neither to eat nor drink until they had killed Paul. There were more than forty who joined in this conspiracy." Because Paul was a Roman citizen, the Roman soldiers protected Paul by moving him to Caesarea at night with a guard of two hundred soldiers, seventy horsemen, and two hundred spearmen. Paul otherwise would have been a "sacrifice" for the group that hated Christians. The earlier vignette of the authoritarian, power-ridden man demanding the resignation of the pastor is representative of this need for the pastor to be "offered up" as a sacrificial lamb.

The Dynamics of Power

The authoritarian, power-ridden person is intoxicated with the love of power. If this hunger for power is to be satisfied in the context of the church, the church must bend to this person's will. The New Testament is a primary document for understanding the dynamics of power. The Greek language is a remarkable source for distinguishing among various meanings of our one English word, *power*. The Greeks used three different words, *dunamis, katakurieuo,* and *eksousia*. Let's look at these three words.

Dunamis

Dunamis refers to the power of God. Paul says in Romans 1:16: "For I am not ashamed of the gospel; it is the power of God for salvation to everyone who has faith, to the Jew first and also to the Greek." Jesus, when talking to Caiaphas the high priest, calls God "the Power" (Matt. 26:64). In many places dunamis is referred to as the power of the Holy Spirit (see Luke 4:14, for example). After his resurrection, Jesus told his disciples, "But you will receive power when the Holy Spirit has come upon you" (Acts 1:8).

These references introduce to our discussion of the struggle between a powerful layperson and a pastor a reality not previously addressed: the presence and power of God. We've been discussing an authoritarian, power-ridden person who thrusts self into total control. This is the subtlest temptation we face—supplanting God. Milton describes this in *Paradise Lost.* Satan is speaking of hell:

> Here we may remain secure; and, in my choice,
> To reign is worth ambition, though in Hell:
> Better to reign in Hell than serve in heaven. (1. 261-63)

In church power struggles, for one person or more self-elevation or *hubris* takes over and the sovereign power of God is forgotten and ignored. Finding a consensus in a community of faith calls for a humbling of the whole congregation, especially those being tempted to take complete control. Friedrich Nietzsche describes this temptation:

> God is dead! God remains dead!
> We have killed him! How shall we console ourselves? . . .
> Shall we not ourselves have to become gods, merely to seem worthy
> of it?[6]

The authoritarian, power-ridden person is intoxicated with power and is, wittingly or not, yielding to the subtlest of all temptations, to try to take God's place. This is a fatal force evident in church conflicts.

Katakurieuo

This leads us to the second Greek word for power, *katakurieuo*. It means "to become master, gain dominion over, gain power over someone or something." In Matthew 20:25 Jesus told his disciples,

> You know that the rulers of the Gentiles lord it over them, and their great ones are tyrants over them. It will not be so among you; but whoever wishes to be great among you must be your servant, and whoever wishes to be first among you must be your slave; just as the Son of Man came not to be served but to serve, and to give his life a ransom for many.

In 1 Peter 5:3 the elders are admonished not to "lord it over" those in
their charge but to "be examples to the flock." Even among Jesus'
disciples there were struggles for power. They asked him, "Who is
the greatest in the kingdom of heaven?" (Matt. 18:1). James and
John asked him, "Grant us to sit, one at your right hand and one at
your left, in your glory" (Mark 10:37).

These struggles for power have been evident in the divisions of the
church throughout history. The sons of Zebedee made no room for the
other ten disciples. One can assume that they envisioned the other ten as
their subordinates. Again, Jesus likened their concern to Gentile rulers
who lord it over others. In contrast, Jesus came not to be served but to
serve and give his life as a ransom for many. He is our model for service, not the Gentile rulers.

Eksousia

This is a third New Testament word for power. It is used to mean the
power exercised by rulers and their jurisdictions, such as Herod's juris-
diction in Luke 4:6. But its primary meanings are "freedom of choice or
a right; an ability or a capability." In Matthew 28:18 the word refers to
the absolute authority or power of the resurrected Christ as he commis-
sioned his disciples to go and make disciples of all nations. In John 1:12
eksousia refers to the ability, power, or strength to become the children
of God "who were born, not of blood or of the will of the flesh or of the
will of man, but of God."

God, the ultimate source of spiritual energy, energizes us. This
energy comes through our belief in the Christ. It enables growth in the
spirit as we become the children of God.

Yet the whole teaching of the New Testament says that this *becoming* is in the context of the family of God. We are not orphans, desolate
in an impersonal world. As Jesus said in John 14:18, 23, "I will not
leave you orphaned. . . . Those who love me will keep my word, and my
Father will love them, and we will come to them and make our home
with them."

The home we have is the family of God in Jesus Christ. We dwell together as a fellowship of believers who do not lord it over one another. We iron out our difficulties with each other on a face-to-face basis. We do not give up on one another or exclude one another. In our churches today, ministers earn a wage from the church and can be "fired," a condition alien to the early church. They did not have this structural dependency. We have a structural dependency of pastors who are pushed into inauthenticity by their fear of the congregation.

But when a pastor is confronted by an authoritarian, power-ridden church member, her major recourse is the teachings of Jesus in Matthew 5:23-24 and 18:15. These passages deserve repetition because they are so important in the care of troublesome people:

> Matthew 5:23-24: So when you are offering your gift at the altar, if you remember that your brother or sister has something against you, leave your gift there before the altar and go; first be reconciled to your brother or sister, and then come and offer your gift.

> Matthew 18:15: If another member of the church sins against you, go and point out the fault when the two of you are alone. If the member listens to you, you have regained that one.

Individual churches and larger judicatories continually reverse the process Jesus taught. They begin with a personal attack on someone in the presence of the whole church or convention, continue with a committee assigned to consider the charges, and may never get to the face-to-face, one-on-one conversation between the accused and the accuser. Worse than this, they may begin with a personal attack published in the religious journals or the secular newspapers or reported on television. In the pattern of reconciliation Jesus taught, one can hope for the promising outcome: "If two of you agree on earth about anything you ask, it will be done for you by my Father in heaven. For where two or three are gathered in my name, I am there among them" (Matt. 18:19-20).

The authoritarian, power-ridden man or woman is terrified by such face-to-face, one-on-one relationships. As I have said before, this person needs an audience to divide and conquer. Care of these people begins in the privacy of a face-to-face effort to get them to listen and be reconciled. The compassionate provision of privacy gives them an unexpected freedom from embarrassment. It allows them no audience to exploit.

"For God is a God not of disorder but of peace" (1 Cor. 14:33). This approach takes courage.

Congregations are rarely aware of these explicit teachings of Jesus. At a time of relative peace in the church, a pastor can teach them in small discussion groups. Group discussions allow for conversation and not just the one-way communication of a sermon. But a pastor might also preach on these texts.

Then if an individual subsequently asks for the pastor's resignation, she can be asked, "Have you and the pastor had a private conversation about this?" If the answer is no, the moderator can turn to the teachings of Jesus and say, "This matter must be discussed between the two of you first. If you can't come to an agreement, then another person can be asked to sit with the two of you. If it cannot be resolved this way, then and only then will it be in order for this matter to be discussed in an open business meeting."

Through such preaching, discussing, and modeling, the authoritarian, power-ridden person is faced with the teachings of One whose power puts human power plays under the discipline of the authority of God. The whole congregation will also be nudged to remember the teachings of the Lord Jesus Christ. In the end, the pastor and the authoritarian person will become more authentic as leaders in the church.

CHAPTER 4

The Care of the Competitive Divider of the Congregation

Competition in the Early Church

Competition among congregational members has been with the Christian community since the beginning. Paul describes it in 1 Corinthians 3:3-6:

> For as long as there is jealousy and quarreling among you, are you not of the flesh, and behaving according to human inclinations? For when one says, "I belong to Paul," and another, "I belong to Apollos," are you not merely human?
>
> What then is Apollos? What is Paul? Servants through whom you came to believe, as the Lord assigned to each. I planted, Apollos watered, but God gave the growth.

Elsewhere, in 1 Corinthians 9:24-27, Paul uses athletic figures of speech to describe the healthy place of competition in the Christian community: "Do you not know that in a race the runners all compete, but only one receives the prize? Run in such a way that you may win it. Athletes exercise self-control in all things. . . . " Then in 2 Timothy 2:5 the athletic metaphor is again used: "And in the case of an athlete, no one is crowned without competing according to the rules."

Obviously, competition is of two kinds. One divides a congregation into competitive camps, led by competing leaders, splitting the congregation. It sets people over against one another and divides the community of faith. An example of this in the early church was the schism over whether Gentile converts had to be circumcised. Paul and Peter opposed each other over this, as we discussed earlier. Yet they dealt with each other face to face. The church as a whole solved the problem and the competition at the Jerusalem conference (see Acts 15).

The other kind of competition unifies the people of God—as they compete "according to the rules." In the Christian faith we seek an imperishable prize and discipline our competitive spirit so that "after proclaiming to others I myself should not be disqualified" (1 Cor. 9:27). The unified congregation competes together for the imperishable blessing of God in Jesus Christ. Paul states it most succinctly in Romans 12:10: "Love one another with mutual affection; outdo one another in showing honor."

So in the New Testament, the problems of competition were of two kinds: the kind that divides the church, as with Apollos and Paul in the Corinthian church, and the kind where competitors "outdo one another in showing honoring." In the latter contest of kindness, everybody wins.

Competition in the Contemporary Church

In the contemporary church, competition tends to be measured in terms of success—in terms of the number of followers a person can gather; the amount of prestige a given individual has in the eyes of followers; the degree of superiority in these respects one has over one's chief competitors.

Several examples make this kind of competition more vivid. A Methodist church had a separate building for a men's Bible class—more than one hundred men, most of whom rarely attended the worship hour led by the pastor. The class teacher was a prominent businessman, and his students were mostly other business and professional men. A garage mechanic, a mill hand, or other "blue collar" person, though welcome, would have felt out of place. In this example I see competition on two levels—between the Sunday school teacher and the pastor and also among professional men who did not mingle with outsiders.

Another, similar example: A Sunday school class taught by a prominent lawyer had built a log cabin meeting room on the church grounds. They had an unspoken competitive relationship with the pastor who led the morning worship service. This was intensified by the fact that the class teacher was the son of the founding pastor of the church. The teacher was the extended presence of his father, now deceased.

A third example of competitive behavior clearly divided a church: The church staff included a children's minister, a youth minister, and a minister of education, each having a loyal following in the congregation. These staff members were alienated from the pastor because they and their baby-boomer followers wanted a less formal and more flexible, enthusiastic, and contemporary worship service. They also felt that the pastor should resign. A few lay leaders of Sunday school classes felt the same way. This church division—of which many heavy financial contributors were unaware—was particularly intense because a division similar in both content and staff alignment had resulted in the departure of two previous pastors. The pastor saw the present situation as a repetition of the pattern of disloyalty to and competition with the pastor. He felt that these staff members wanted to *be* the pastor! They, in turn, insisted that they expected him to be a good administrator as well as a "contemporary" worship leader.

An outside observer who knew this church staff well saw a common characteristic in all the competitive parties—an intense anxiety and low-level depression.

In such a situation, "boundaries" have never been clearly defined and mutually agreed upon, or they are ignored. Some people are unaware of where they leave off and other people "take up." They are equally unaware of the conflict they create. Other people are exceptionally defensive of their "territory" and guard their turf jealously. The task of a pastor is to blow the whistle when a member of the staff team is "off-side." To do so is to care for the whole team.

Competition that leads to divisiveness is like drinking salt water; it provides wetness without slaking the thirst. It makes the thirsty all the more thirsty.

A widely known contemporary example of competitiveness that has led to divisiveness is the deliberate efforts of fundamentalists to "take over" the Southern Baptist Convention. As a professor in the Department of Psychiatry at the University of Louisville, I have not been involved in this conflict between the fundamentalists and the moderates. The people hurt by this twelve-year competition are those who have been life-long Southern Baptists—the second-, third-, and fourth-generation Southern Baptists. I did not become aware of "the Convention" until I was a second-year student at the Southern Baptist Theological Seminary. I have been a faithful listener and comforter to those whose families have invested themselves in the Convention for generations. Over the years, I have seen the severe grief of people who consider such competitiveness to be ethically wrong. They see the political tactics of the "take-over" strategists to be breaking the rules of godly competition—to outdo one another in showing honor, to desecrate one another or eliminate people from jobs because someone disagrees with them. It remains to be seen whether or not these competitors will eventually divide themselves—turn against one another. Competitiveness of this kind is a way of life.

Such denominational divisions are not unique to Southern Baptists. Other denominations are severely divided with competitive leaders—the moving spirits of differing factions. Sometimes they "compete according to the rules" of "outdoing one another in showing honor." Much of the time they do not. Even the most worthy causes, such as the rights of women and homosexuals or the protection of uncertified immigrants, can be led by leaders determined to win by whatever means are possible. In fact, competing leaders of worthy causes can collide with one another for the leadership of the same cause.

And protagonists of either side of an ideological cause may "use" the pastor, lay leaders, and the church as a platform for their cause without concern for the possible division and/or destruction of the integrity of the church.

Some Dynamics of Competition

In caring for the competitive spirit, you might look for the following dynamics. These insights might lead you to an avenue of empathic understanding.

Sibling Rivalry

The forces of competition are driven by many psychosocial energies. People with family histories of sibling rivalry may be highly competitive. Biblical personalities immediately come to mind: Cain and Abel, Jacob and Esau, the Elder Brother and the Prodigal Son. Though not brothers, David and Saul were competitive to the nth degree.

Social Class

Another source of competitive behavior is a person's social-class back-
ground. If someone grew up in a low economic class and has by sheer
intelligence and hard work climbed the ladder to one of the professions
or to exceptional business success, the habits of competitiveness will
most likely be brought to church. For example, competition can show its
head if a person of elite heritage and "old family" breeding is appointed
as a committee chair instead of a "self-made" man or woman. The self-
made individual may feel excluded and offended and attract followers
who form a division in the church.

Contending Families

Many churches, particularly small congregations, are made up of just a
few families. I live and work in Kentucky. I have been pastor of two
churches, one rural and one urban. They were alike, however, in that the
membership was dominated by a few families. The competition between
these families was intense. In the rural church, families had grudges
against other families. The smallest issue could quickly divide them
along family lines. In recent history, Kentucky "clan" culture has become more a war of words than of guns.

Pastor-Staff Conflicts

In a multiple-staff church, staff members may be in divisive competition
with one another. As previously discussed, the children's minister, the
youth minister, and the minister of education may each develop his or
her own "church within a church." Though the three may be at peace
with the others, each might have a personal following and this loyalty
can cause competition within the congregation. In the example earlier in
the chapter, they all agreed that the pastor was inadequate and should be
dismissed. Their competitiveness with him further divided the church.

Pastoral Antipathy to Administration

A pastor who is absorbed in preaching and pastoral care but abhors the executive administration of the church leaves a leadership vacuum. Laypeople and/or staff members will move into the administrative tasks. They may compete with one another for the leadership of various functions. The pastor may then become alarmed that these people are trying to "take over." The pastor may or may not be aware of having neglected these administrative functions.

Disdain for administrative tasks is often learned in seminary. Many professors tend verbally to disparage the tasks of "bureaucracy," and yet many are eager to take on such tasks in the school because administrative jobs pay more, provide secretarial help and computers, and are wrongly seen as more prestigious than teaching.

In spite of actions of former professors, an effective pastor sees the congregation as a caring system. This involves approaching administrative tasks as being a form of *caring* for individual people as interlocking members of a network that makes up the system as a whole. This pastor begins to think of administration as a shepherding of the whole system as a living organism. The apostle Paul speaks of the church as the body of Christ with many members in the one body. Each part has need of all the others. Competition is according to the rules of Christ who is the head (see 1 Cor. 12). The church system is alive, with each member working with and for the rest of the members. They bear one another's burdens. They fulfill the law of Christ. Jesus said, "I give you a new commandment, that you love one another. Just as I have loved you, you also should love one another" (John 13:34). This love is expressed in a community of faith in which members outdo one another in showing honor. Such care is competing "according to the rules"—bearing one another's burden of fault and weakness and caring for one another as Jesus Christ cared for us. So in the fellowship of believers, confrontation is transformed into a spirit of gentleness and restoration. Our anger is expressed as pain and hurt, and our words become conciliatory instead of harsh and punitive. As pastors you might consider administration as the art of reconciliation—encouraging members to restore one another in a spirit of gentleness (see Gal. 6:1). These are "the rules" of the competition at work in the community of faith.

These rules are rarely invoked in the competitive "rat race" of the busy church in which destructive competition breaks all the rules. Even worse than this, the congregation as a whole system working together does not *know* what the rules are. They innately *feel* it when they break the rules or are victimized by others breaking the rules. But *feeling* injustice is far short of knowing how the scriptures put the rules into words and actions.

Preventing and Caring about Staff Competition

This discussion of competing in the Christian fellowship "according to the rules" provides some questions about caring for competitors who potentially or actually divide the congregation and set Christians over against one another. How is this care given first by the congregation and then by the pastor?

Preventing Competition among Staff Members

The first task of the congregation in caring for the competitive divider is to set limits beyond which a competitor may not go in terms of divisive behaviors. As the song says, it's best to "start at the very beginning." Some suggestions for preventing competition when hiring paid personnel:

A church with a multiple staff needs a personnel committee with the task of matching the gifts of a prospective staff member with the expectations of the congregation. Those expectations (a job description) should be written down and made known to the congregation and to the applicant. Many collisions with competitive personalities can be prevented if a clearly and mutually understood covenant is made *in writing* at the very outset. It is especially important that new staff members know to whom they are answerable. In addition, the supervising party should carry out this role by being in regular contact with those answerable to her.

Every paid minister needs a job description. This should be thought through before someone is interviewed. In a personnel interview, the first order of business is to ask the applicant what his or her dreams or expectations are. Then explain the job description. If the person's expectations far exceed the responsibilities he or she will have, the applicant might prove to be competitive, wanting to move into other people's territory.

Recruiting and Orienting New Staff Members

The personnel committee might well explore an applicant's commitment to the pastor, the staff member ultimately responsible for staffing. Before being hired, applicants need to get acquainted with the pastor in an interview in which mutual expectations are compared.

If this is an entry-level position, the supervisor does well to orient the new staff member during the first month and continue in weekly supervisory conferences as a regular discipline. In exceptionally large churches, the supervisor may be a minister of administration. In such churches, the pastor tends to serve as the chief executive officer. A staff can easily become a competitive group. The pastor and/or the minister of administration is responsible for seeing the very earliest signs of staff competitions, especially those that have the potential for dividing the congregation. The staff members themselves should observe the "rule" of outdoing each other in showing honor to one another. When staff members start demeaning and putting one another down, the pastor and/ or the administrator should intervene and prevent competitive division or "ganging up" in a clique against the rest of the staff and/or the pastor. This should be "nipped in the bud" and such competitors should be restored in a spirit of gentleness and self-examination (see Gal. 6:1). This becomes the "rule" by which normal competition can be kept within bounds.

Competitiveness in the Congregation

Laypeople themselves are tempted to become competitive dividers of the congregation. This is true in congregations of all sizes today. The competition tends to form along generational lines. People born before the Great Depression and World War II tend to have dramatically different values from those born since 1948. These differences are made very clear in Robert Bellah's *Habits of the Heart*.[1] These differences can cause competition and division.

The different understandings of worship, for example, can easily divide a congregation into separate competing "churches" within a church. The younger group generally prefers contemporary music heavily influenced by Christian rock musicians. Many enjoy worshipping with bodily movement and applause—spontaneity in the service. The older group expects music from the hymn book, a more formal order of service, and maybe the traditional "Rite One" service from the Episcopal *Book of Common Prayer.*

The issue of inclusive language in worship can become divisive if the leadership is competitive and divisive. A group's personal attachment to the traditional hymns, readings, and biblical texts needs to be considered in the decision making. These matters should be dealt with by a task force of wise and gentle people.

Congregations need to anticipate, prevent, and/or heal competitive divisions. There is potential for a competitive spirit in the election of the diaconate, the session, the vestry, or a similar church board and in the choosing of the chair of powerful committees, such as finance, personnel, and nominating committees. (Each denomination has a different name for these committees, but basic functions involve managing money, managing personnel, and appointing members to standing committees and *ad hoc* committees.) In congregational churches, a pastoral search committee can easily "break" into competing factions; in a hierarchical system this might happen with a pastoral negotiating team.

These key issues provide the congregational arena in which competitive and divisive influences play out their acts. I have just conferred with a retired and disabled pastor friend, the pastor of three large churches for thirteen years each. I asked him where competitive divisions in these churches were most evident. He replied, "In the competition for places of leadership." The politics of church leadership and influence are reflected in Paul's comment: "Do you not know that all the runners compete, but only one receives the prize?" (1 Cor. 9:24). In church races people not appointed can become disgruntled and gather around themselves followers, creating a church within a church. They might even pull out and start an entirely separate church.

Pastoral Leadership in Caring for Competitive, Divisive Persons

The pastor is the overseer (*episcopos*) of the flock I have just described. The guardian of the unity of the system of the church. Wherever people are, competition abounds. The pastor "sees to it that" (one translation of the verb *episkopeo*) the competition is within the boundaries of the rules of "the law of Christ" (Gal. 6:2).

To pastors and lay leaders, I suggest the following ways of doing this:

Being Sensitive

It is important to be sensitive to the disappointment of people not appointed to positions they had hoped to hold. You can come alongside these people and encourage them to pour out their feelings of disappointment. Gently restore them by affirming their true gifts; covenant to work toward finding a place in the church for their expression of those gifts. Enable them to vent with you their feelings of injustice if they feel someone has wronged them. If they feel a particular person has offended them, encourage them to talk privately with that person. If the two cannot come to an understanding, you might offer to talk with the two of them together, to work toward peace and reconciliation.

Exploring Dreams and Aspirations

A wise pastor takes advantage of the "runaway creativity" in the competitive, divisive person. This person's dreams and aspirations need to be guided by a caring overseer.

Why do I use the term *runaway creativity*? Sometimes the competitive person is reacting "creatively" to an unidentified problem. For example, let's say someone starts a clique that pulls out and forms another congregation. This act may point out that the original congregation was too large. The Hutterites have ritualized an answer to this. A church community deliberately sets aside money, and as their numbers increase, they take the fund and buy a "stake" of land to start a new church with new leadership.

A pastor might need to ask whether or not the church has become so large that many talented people are being left out of the leadership. A homely figure of speech says that churches are like beehives. When bees get too crowded, they "swarm" and start a new hive. The wise beekeeper knows this and prepares a hive for the swarming bees.

Competitive energy often can be rechanneled within the congregation. A divorced man who had custody of his children wanted very much to be the finance committee chairman—even though he acknowledged that "math" was not his forte. The man was disappointed when a certified public accountant was appointed instead of him. The pastor, noting that the divorce-recovery group had no leader, suggested that this single father take the leadership of that group. He did so and has done a superb job in that role. Finding a person's special gifts can be an effective way to make the best of "runaway creativity."

The Atmosphere of Competition

American life is saturated with competition. We live in a success-oriented culture, where competition is seen as a key to success. It never occurs to many church members that competition and success can sometimes be wrong.

Competition is the stuff that keeps America going economically. Churches themselves are in persistent competition with one another— even within a denomination—for members, public attention, and funds. The American obsession with success is the outer cover of competition. The heavy emphasis upon positive thinking and possibility thinking makes spiritual discernment about the rules of competition difficult to grasp.

This competition is so subtle and accepted that a pastor may not feel she can deal with the topic directly. Yet a pastor might preach a pair of sermons; one on creative competition, such as the New Testament teaches, and one on destructive competition. A follow-up discussion group for feedback from the congregation would be helpful.

The athletic metaphors of the New Testament provide a good "handle" for preaching or teaching on the ethics of competition, particularly competitiveness in the life of the Christian community. The enchantment of Americans with sports makes the subject relevant to the congregation.

Events in business and politics can provide living sermon illustrations. For example, in the last two months, my county sheriff has been convicted of a felony in handling money, my state's entire lottery board has been fired for misappropriating lottery funds, and the husband of our only female (former) governor was convicted for extorting more than one million dollars from two bond-underwriting firms and tax fraud. In addition, a few months earlier several state legislators were convicted of money and influence crimes. A sermon on competing according to the rules has plenty of illustrations!

But do not pay so much attention to the successes of athletes and the felonies of politicians that you distract the congregation's attention from the divisiveness of unscrupulous competition in the life of the church. When the secular world presents as much unscrupulous competition as I have described, it's easy to divert one's attention from greedy competition in the church. But such competition is as obvious as the nose on your face! But you and I cannot *see* our noses without the help of a mirror! Even then we straightway forget how we look (see James 1:23). We need to edify one another through caring admonitions. We can see the noses on each other's faces. I can remind you of how you look—and you can do the same for me.

CHAPTER 5

The Care of the Clinging Vine or Dependent Person

You are greeting people after the morning service and it happens again. One particular person stops and engages you in a long conversation while other people wait . . . and wait, until they finally give up and leave by another door.

Or just before a congregational gathering, this same person stops you and asks for advice on something you feel a person as old as he could decide for himself. Finally you have to break off the discussion to get the meeting started on time.

Then this person calls you at home more and more often to ask your advice or help in making a decision. Again you think a person "of a certain age" could decide this without your input. Besides, these telephone calls interrupt your private time with your family (or colleagues, as in the case of a celibate pastor). You begin to resent this person as a nuisance, a pest, a bother. You wish this parishioner would go away and leave you alone.

Your impatience seeps through into your conversations with this person. Your tone of voice becomes shrill. Then your anger gets the best of you, and you blast out: "Why do you have to call me so much at inopportune times?"

Then the person takes up another routine: writing you notes of apology, giving gifts to you or members of your family. She wants to do things for you that you would rather do for yourself. This routine taxes your patience until you lose patience again.

In response to this, the person blows up at you: "After all I have done for you, you treat me this way! I was only trying to be helpful!" It is a temper tantrum. Some dependent types, instead of having temper tantrums, will become depressed, withdrawn, and even threaten suicide in a note written to you. *That* will get your "help" when nothing else will.

What on earth is going on here? You have become the object of the dependent member's need for someone else to make his or her decisions. If you as pastor lose patience with him, or he with you, he soon will shift the dependency to another individual or couple. A lay leader and spouse whose children are grown and out of the house (or if the couple has lost a child by death) may actually enjoy this dependency. (Know that the lay leader's opinion of you as a pastor may become colored by the accounts given by this dependent person.)

Some Reasons for Dependency

In caring for dependent people it is helpful to develop some working hypotheses as to how they came to be this way. These hypotheses give you clues for caring. They can also guide you in setting reasonable limits on their manipulation of you.

Early Beginnings—Parental Overprotection

Erik Erikson and others relate dependency to the very earliest beginnings of our lives. He says that this is the stage when trust is formed and hope is kindled. The mother and father provide *everything* for the infant. An infant is a ravenous appetite at one end and total irresponsibility at the other end! If the infant's every need is not met, you're sure to hear about it!

But if these needs for food, cleanliness, and freedom from pain are met and the child is given physical affection and care, the child develops trust in this new and unknown world. Erikson says that faith in God is eventually made of this early, basic trust and hope.

If the person does not build religious faith then he or she "must derive a basic faith from elsewhere."[1] The dependent person seems to invest his basic faith in other humans. Only a few human beings are comfortable being the *center* of another person's life. (There are a few such people around, as evidenced in the authoritarian, power-ridden person.)

Typically, adults "stuck" in the dependent way of life have or had parents who did everything for them. Instead of instilling autonomy and confidence, parents instilled doubt that the growing children could do anything on their own. Parents "micromanaged," telling children what to do about even the most trivial thing. Children grew to adulthood not believing in themselves or their ability to make it on their own.

The foregoing discussion gives one specific insight for caring for dependent people: From the outset, invest confidence in their ability to venture out on their own. For example, instead of making small—or big—decisions for them, outline a number of good and "doable" options. Then say, "I believe you have the ability to decide this for yourself. What do *you* think you will do, or do you want to think about it for a while?"

Dependent people are afraid of responsibility and having the freedom to make their own decisions. They are like the man in Jesus' parable who said to his master, "I was afraid, and I went and hid your talent in the ground" (Matt. 25:25).

Our challenge is to calm their anxieties in the presence of their freedom to decide for themselves. We can listen to their fears and despair and not to their demands. This is one common-sense way of caring for them.

Authoritarian Teaching

As children enter the school and/or the church system, they are at risk for meeting teachers and/or pastors and leaders who insist on making all decisions for them. An example of authoritarian religious thought is the Bill Gothard teachings about the family. Gothard counselors—who can be consulted by long-distance telephone—manage the smallest life details for the family system. The wife is to be subject to the husband; she should teach the children at home, and so forth. I am astonished at how people turn their lives over to these long-distance counselors. A dependency is perpetuated.

In many authoritarian religious groups, followers have been exploited for money. The Jim and Tammy Bakker dynasty is an example. The Jim Jones group followed him in a mass suicide; after the tragic death of more than nine hundred followers, large caches of money, including Social Security checks, were found by authorities.

The Branch Davidians led by David Koresh near Waco, Texas,

provide a more recent example of an extreme authoritarian religious group. Such leaders could not rally a following if there were no dependent personalities. Like sheep led to the slaughter, people turn their lives over to the dictation of one person who makes all their decisions for them.

In encouraging dependent people to think for themselves, we steer clear of authoritarian religious teaching. In some cases a woman sees a biblical basis for being dependent on a man's spiritual direction or authority. But the authoritarianism of men in relation to women overlooks the creation story, which says,

> So God created humankind in his image,
> > in the image of God he created them;
> > male and female he created them. (Gen. 1:27)

This describes a mutual participation in the image of God. No dependence of women is here. And the apostle Paul says, "There is no longer Jew or Greek, there is no longer slave or free, there is no longer male and female; for all of you are one in Christ Jesus" (Gal. 3:28). No dependence here!

Dependency and Pastoral Counseling

A whole generation of pastoral counselors came to maturity under the influence of Carl Rogers, who initially developed his therapy approach with a population of college students struggling to become independent adults, to "individuate" from their parental home. His approach was originally called nondirective counseling and later named client-centered therapy. His objective was to enable his clients to manage their own problems, to encourage them to accept responsibility for their own lives. Rogerian counselors do not provide a solution for problems; they encourage clients to analyze problems and to make decisions of their own.

Rogerian theory emphasizes the importance of seeing counselees— or parishioners—as individuals of worth and significance who have the capacity to deal with their lives and decisions. The counselor finds a client's internal frame of reference by creating an atmosphere of warmth and acceptance. Rogers says we counselors must put aside ourselves to the best of our ability. To the counselee we become "a safe opportunity for you [the counselee] to discern yourself more clearly, to experience yourself more truly and deeply, to choose more significantly."[2]

Rogerian theory is vividly relevant to the pastoral care of dependent people. In Rogers's schema, these people have only a superficial desire for us to make their decisions for them. They are really struggling for independence and then interdependence. Note a much more recent comment from another source: "the sufferer is yearning to be listened to, to be valued and to be understood. . . the attentive listening of a concerned and interested healer can, and often does, have a compelling effect on the sufferer."[3]

I give the example of a part-time minister to youth in a large semi-rural church. One of her volunteer leaders insisted on talking with her endlessly after the evening youth meeting. The late hours began to wear on the minister's nerves. Finally she invited the woman to visit her in the nearby city where she had an office. She hoped they could talk when they both would be rested and have no distractions. She made it clear, and the woman agreed, that this would be a formal counseling situation.

She let the woman talk and pour out her concerns, which included a deeply held confession of what she felt made her feel ashamed and unworthy. They worked over the issues of God's forgiveness and restoration. She was assured of God's forgiveness and her worthiness to be a youth leader. They celebrated in prayer together. She was not as dependent as she was anxious and guilt laden.

If someone keeps crowding you for time and hindering your public ministry, look on this as a cry for help. Arrange a time and place of discreet privacy and listen closely. This person may carry a burden that has never been shared with anyone. He may not be dependent at all but a conscience-stricken person seeking someone who will listen, understand, and lead him to hope in the forgiveness of God.

Do You Have the Time?

But, you will say, I don't have the time to schedule two, three, or four
hour-long appointments with a clinging-vine, dependent person. My
response? You don't have the time not to do so! This person will use up
that much time snatching brief, frustrating conversations with you. This
parishioner is in charge of the situation, and you are the captive.

When you structure the time and place of your care, you are in control and can guide and sustain this person without interruptions by others
and without feeling trapped. In fact, you will probably use less time
taking this tack than any other. You will certainly be less likely to blow
your stack.

Many pastors do not set specific counseling times for parishioners;
they reason that they cannot do this for *all* their church members so they
shouldn't do it for any. But all do not want or need such attention. And
many will appreciate the difference the counseling is making in the lives
of one or more very anxious people. In addition to preaching, visiting
the sick, conducting funerals, and officiating at weddings, you have set
aside some carefully planned time for a person in need. You have met
him or her in your office at the church or in your study at home—with a
secretary, lay leader, or at least one family member present outside your
office or study. This attendant ground rule applies to counselees of both
genders.

The fear of being accused of sexual harassment may keep you from
seeing privately a counselee of the opposite gender. This is a legitimate
concern, but one that can be resolved if you limit your bodily contact to
handshakes. Also, avoid meetings outside your office and sessions held
during lunch and—God forbid—dinner.

If indeed the person begins to interpret your work together in a
romantic or seductive way, remind the parishioner that this time is for
serious work on his or her need to grow; unrealistic romance changes the
subject. To yield to this kind of pressure is a misuse of the power of
your office as pastor or church leader. You can clearly define the limits
of your *role*, fix the time of meeting when others are in the area, keep the
place of meeting unchanged, and refrain from self-disclosure of personal
problems of your own. This way you are sticking to the *work* of caring
for the parishioner. You can further protect the counselee and yourself
from confused, anxious involvement with each other: If the person will

not abide by these instructions, you can refer him to a pastoral counseling center, clinical psychologist, or psychiatrist.

Some pastors avoid counseling parishioners for a third reason: Not feeling qualified in "pastoral psychotherapy," they prefer referring people to pastoral care specialists who have had extensive training in counseling and different forms of psychotherapy. These professionals often work in counseling centers geographically apart from the church.

In its infancy, "pastoral counseling" was practiced and sponsored by preaching pastors such as Leslie Weatherhead, Harry Emerson Fosdick, John Sutherland Bonnell, Norman Vincent Peale, and Theodore F. Adams. Later its practice was relocated to the hospital chaplaincy by persons such as Anton Boisen, Russell Dicks, and Richard Cabot. Now the American Association of Pastoral Counselors (AAPC) is vigorously involved in efforts to receive government recognition, so members would be classified as health care deliverers whose services would be eligible for insurance coverage. Very few churches financially support them, and they are pushed to charge fees, get insurance payments, and so forth. This shift of focus away from church-based counseling is being corrected by a few churches that are establishing their own counseling services. Some of these churches pay the counselors a salary and receive all fees as a gift to the church. A few churches pay salaries and charge no fees. This is the most effective way to go. Other churches provide the office space and receptionist service and take a percentage of fees in return, varying 40 percent down to 10 percent. In effect, these counselors are in a quasiprivate practice in the locale of the church. If they are members of the AAPC, they are required to have malpractice insurance. Still, should a malpractice suit be filed, it would likely name the church as a codefendant.

This intensive discussion of professional pastoral counseling as a specialty has been generated from the issue of pastors not having time to give to time-consuming counseling. How the pastoral counseling specialist is to make a living is relevant to pastors making referrals. The churches often accept no financial responsibility for supporting the pastoral care specialist. They exercise no oversight with a system of supervision and answerability to the church. The subtle secularization of much pastoral counseling is the result. As Robert Coles, professor of psychiatry and humanities at Harvard, says, clergy "should not see their work [as being] too professional or specialized. The hazard is to become too intellectualized or psychologically oriented—no longer to think of your ministry as a ministry of service. Instead you become a therapist."[4] Faithful, hard-working members of the Association of Pastoral Counselors are, with some success, reversing this secularization. Still, individual churches are slow to be of much assistance to them.

I see another concern when the dependent person is referred to a pastoral counseling specialist who charges fees. It's possible that affluent people might be recommended an endless series of interviews with no operative treatment plan. A counselee may become "addicted" to the process of interview after interview, and the counselor may become financially dependent on the counselee. High-paying clients can have their dependency needs met and not be encouraged to change. As the IRS man in the Ziggy cartoon says: "No, Mr. Ziggy, you cannot list your psychiatrist as a dependent!"

I propose the following pattern for preventing clients from becoming too dependent on counselors. The counselor needs to part of an ongoing peer group that meets at least once a week. In this group counselors present case material for peer review.

1. With a new client, the first eight interviews would be at the counselor's own discretion.

2. At the end of the eighth interview, the counselor would present the case to the peer group along with a diagnosis and a plan of treatment.

3. At the end of the twentieth interview, the case should be presented again to the group to decide whether to proceed much further or to begin a referral process to seek outside consultation. This would be to seek collaboration with a clinical psychologist or a psychiatrist who practices psychotherapy and is not simply a dispenser of medication. (The practitioners of hospital psychiatry too often ask social workers, nurses, or pastoral counselors to do the work of psychotherapy and/or family therapy. The psychiatrist too often deals only with the medication and hospitalization of the patient, focusing on diagnosis, the prescription of drugs, and the medical check-ups on the course of medications.)

Conclusion

Let us conclude this chapter by returning to the discussion of the busy pastor of a congregation. You and your lay leaders have an opportunity to affect the process of care for the dependent person—or for anyone else, for that matter. If you plan to spend from one to five interviews with someone in need, explain this time frame to the parishioner. Then explore the depths of the present despair and the shape of the person's hopes for the future. You can often satisfy the person's need for attention. You can invest confidence in the person's ability to make decisions. You can be a Barnabas, a son or daughter of encouragement.

At the end of a few interviews and assessment, you turn to a network of professionals for referrals, depending on potential problems you see. You might rely on a ready-made network of church members who are professionals—internists and family practice physicians, lawyers, social workers, pastoral counselors, chaplains, and psychiatrists. You can add to this network professionals in the larger community. If you have made it your business to develop such a network, these professionals will become a system of caretakers who come alongside you in the care of your flock.

These few counseling sessions have the potential for effecting great change in the parishioner. Even if change is slow and comes through some channel other than you, the sessions give you personal insight and knowledge of the inner world of the dependent person. After having given such personal and private attention, continue to speak briefly to this person in the course of ordinary church activities. Always encourage his ability to be independent. The conversation is a brief follow-up of the steadfast understanding you have together. You have dropped into step alongside this person in a long pilgrimage into maturity under the tutelage of and dependence on the wisdom of God in Christ through the Holy Spirit.

We began this chapter with people who become pests and nuisances. We conclude with people who believe in themselves and trust God. We can listen for the still, small voice that says, "Well done, good and faithful servant."

CHAPTER 6

The Care of the Star Performer

Last Sunday morning during the sermon I noticed that the dais or platform was empty except for the pastor. A single spotlight accentuated his presence at the pulpit and the open Bible.

In most churches many other people want to share that spotlight. Some try to grab the attention as frequently as they can. They are non-professional actors who become a part of the drama at every given opportunity.

It is not by chance that many world-star entertainers get their start at church. This is not evil or bad in its own right. Yet some people with this penchant can be troublesome to pastors and lay leaders. They call for special understanding and care, which we will discuss in this chapter.

At the outset, let me refer you to a previous book of my own; in *Behind the Masks: Personality Disorders in Religious Behaviors*, I said that the *troublesome* star performer is suffering from a histrionic personality disorder.[1] The word *histrionic* comes from the Latin word *histrios*, which means "actor." Life itself, according to Shakespeare, is a stage: "All the world is a stage, and all men and women merely players. And one man in his time plays many parts, his acts being seven ages." Shakespeare then lists each age, from infancy to old age.[2]

In the life of a church, many audiences provide star performers an opportunity to shine—Sunday school classes, youth groups, committees, and so forth. Not all acting, drama, and work in the spotlight is bad. If somebody is disciplined in the art of drama and *steadfast* and dependable and has integrity, you've got a real asset to the church. And if you think of it, most actors or actresses are team players who readily mesh their parts in with those of others on the stage. But the disordered histrionic individual, our concern here, is that star performer who ignores fellow participants in the life of the church, the community of faith. This person is fickle, short-tempered, and inappropriately situated. An example is the loud choir member who overwhelms all others in the choir. These people are the despair of the minister of music.

A second criterion for separating the legitimate dramatist from the star performer is the person's *steadfastness*. Some people have the capacity to stick productively with the task whether or not the crowd is applauding. They have durable, faithful relationships. The troublesome star performer is oblivious to fidelity and loyalty to co-workers and the common good of the church as a whole. As we shall see, working with star performers, your challenge is to expect and encourage steadfastness and durability of relationship.

I see a third characteristic of troublesome star performers. They generally need superficial excitement; they are easily bored. Anything serious is a "turn off." Anything that is fun or exciting "turns them on." Star performers lead a "turn on—turn off" way of life! For this reason they capture a religious group's attention, but they offer superficiality that is empty of meaningful discourse.

Some Reasons for Being a Star Performer

To understand and develop a measure of empathy for the star performer, one needs to look at this person's history and heritage as well as the present situation.

"Show and Tell" Parents

Frequently star performers were reared by parents who—from the earliest years—pushed them into beauty pageants and/or competitive and academic achievement. Then in social gatherings, the parents play "show and tell," putting the children on display and telling what great achievers they are. This sets up a habitual pattern of seeking the center of a crowd's attention.

Unstable Child Care

Another childhood pattern characteristic of the star performer is being handed from one person to another for care. With no consistent, reliable relationship provided by any one person, the child was forced to form superficial relationships to many caretakers. The child learned to survive by "putting on a show" for the caretaker here today but gone tomorrow.

A variation on this phenomenon is the child of parents who themselves are in the public eye—politicians, ministers, actors, and the like. A child can become a "scene stealer," a "ham" actress; the "audience" becomes the child's caretaker! Star performing becomes a way of life. Again, these are momentary and superficial "contacts." Theodore Millon says that histrionic people are "lacking in fidelity and loyalty." I would add durability. Millon describes these people as "other directed." They get their cues and satisfaction from the crowd. As Millon says: " . . . cut off from external supplies . . . [they] are likely to engage in a frantic search for stimulation and approval or to become dejected and forlorn."[3]

Children raised to play to a crowd can grow into adults with a religious experience that takes cyclical, fickle shape; it moves from one dramatic event to another: Easter, Christmas, the inauguration of a new pastor, farewells to departing staff members, and other dramatic occasions. Each of these events in the life of the church has its own particular spotlight. The star performers cannot resist a spotlight and must get in it. In doing so, they can create pain and aggravation for pastors and lay leaders.

The Star Performer's Boredom and Subsequent Demands on a Pastor

For a variety of reasons, star performers are prone to be easily bored. They need excitement, no matter how shallow it may be. They want exciting sermons—sermons that entertain and amuse; otherwise, they are bored. These people's attention span is short. They read very little. They spend a great deal of time watching television, big-screen movies, and video tapes and listening to audio tapes. This boredom is characteristic of more and more seminary students, which suggests that more of our future pastors will be histrionic star performers themselves. Yet they face an uncertain future because regardless of how much they try to entertain their audiences, the people soon tire of them, become bored with them, and want a new pastor. In with the new, out with the old.

Soren Kierkegaard said that "Boredom is the root of all evil. In choosing a governess, one, therefore, takes into account not only her sobriety, her faithfulness, and her competence, but also her . . . qualifications for amusing the children." To Kierkegaard the star performer would be "the apostle of empty enthusiasm."[4] A pastor is no governess and the star performer is no child, and yet the star performer expects such "amusement" from the pastor.

Star performers often live out their boredom by criticizing the work of their pastor who is in the spotlight every Sunday and at other times during the week.

The star performer, when placed in the audience, judges the pastor by her ability to amuse and entertain the congregation. If the star performer is able to gather a following, such a group may become an effective force in seeing to it that a pastor is dismissed. (This effort itself provides superficial stimulation for the bored star performer.)

This theme of boredom is further evidenced in congregations today by their preference for frenzied contemporary music and "Christian entertainers." The pastor who ignores or becomes a crusader against this entertainment sets himself up to be rejected. If you have not felt comfortable with such music, I suggest you go to a music or book store and read some of the lyrics of this music. Some of it reflects profound wisdom. I particularly like an older song by Simon and Garfunckel titled "Bridge over Troubled Waters." The singer promises to lay himself down and be a bridge over troubled waters. Not a bad metaphor! This music is old enough that a listener can understand the clearly enunciated words. Much music today sacrifices clarity to loud, screaming volume. Your only recourse is to read the lyrics. This way you can get in touch with the under forty-five segment of your congregation without becoming a star performer yourself.

All of this points to the fact that the pastor over the age of fifty is an endangered species. Many people under that age want to be amused. Neil Postman in his book *Amusing Ourselves to Death: Public Discourse in the Age of Show* comments on religious television shows:

> On television, religion . . . is presented as entertainment. Everything that makes religion an historic, profound, and sacred human activity is stripped away. . . . The preacher is tops. God comes out as second banana. They offer people what they want. Moses, Jesus, Mohammed offer them what they need.[5]

Postman does not go further and point out that these television drama-
tics are repeated again and again in locally televised services of megachurches. Even in smaller churches, worship tends to be shaped to
amuse and entertain. This plays right into the needs of star performers—
as pastors and as parishioners.

When the Pastor and the Church Are Star Performers

The ministry, itself, attracts many star performers. These people are
"just what a congregation is looking for," says the pulpit search committee. Committees negotiating with a district superintendent or a diocesan
bishop for a pastor frequently request someone who is gregarious and
outgoing, a "people person," and especially someone who is "good with
the youth." They do not look for someone who is steadfast in tough
times, who keeps promises, forms clear covenants with a congregation,
and never lets the congregation forget these covenants.

When responding to the star-performer candidate, the committee and
congregation are "swept off their feet." During the first few months
things go well, until the highly dramatic preacher throws a tantrum when
things do not go his way or the minister of music demands too much time
in morning worship. The star-performer pastor wants to make changes
very quickly. To her the old is boring. This pastor or minister of music
craves new things and tires of them almost as quickly as they are
adopted.

If we look at a star performer from a systemic point of view, we see
that the church as a whole has a desire to be a "star" in the community-
at-large. The church is ambitious to have a pastor and a program that
will draw people from other churches as well as people who have no
church at all.

Many churches think they want to become megachurches, where
bigger is better. Such a church majors in quantity of members—five,
ten, or twenty thousand—and superficiality of belief and commitment.
Most have no real tracking system allowing them to stay in touch with
members; fidelity and loyalty is tested only at new-budget time. The
drama and stimulation of the services is what keeps members active and
alert. New people get considerable attention. Many are funneled into
small groups where they can find some sense of continuity and spiritual
identity and personal relationships.

Even ambitious building programs can be a sign of a church wanting the spotlight. This is reminiscent of the story of the Tower of Babel in Genesis 11:1-9. The people of the day said, "Come, let us build ourselves a city, and a tower with its top in the heavens, and let us make a name for ourselves." They were star performers!

Star-performer congregations *need* star-performer pastors. The stimulating and dramatic worship services keep the pastor from being bored. He—and these pastors are traditionally men, with the notable exception of Aimee Semple McPherson of a generation ago—makes a vast drama of preaching. He pitches his own emotions and those of the audience to a shimmering climax. Here is the star at its brightest.

Lloyd Rediger describes the process of becoming a star. The person keeps adding stresses to his or her life and "has a life-style of poor stress management." Stars allow "their primary intimate relationship, usually marriage, to deteriorate until it is no longer supportive." They lose "spiritual commitment and discipline." In this way, "a star is born."[6] At this point in a pastor's pilgrimage, he or she is most vulnerable to severe impaired judgment in one or all of these areas: family life, money management, and/or acting out sexually.

If you are a fellow pastor reading these pages, join me in self-examination, taking a close look at our own star-performer needs. This is a discipline alongside caring for parishioners who complicate life. As we examine ourselves and our congregations, we nurture the empathy needed to care for the star performers among our people.

Keys to Caring for Star Performers

Are We Playing to the Crowd?

If you as pastor and lay leaders are in the swing of an effort to amuse and entertain the congregation, you are probably confirming the star-performer tendencies of such people in your midst. You will have opportunities to "use" star performers in the carefully choreographed "show" of the church. People will come to the church in great numbers to be entertained by entertainers.

You can see that I perceive superficiality and shallowness in this approach to church life. I liken it to what Isaiah says:

[They] say to the seers, "Do not see";
>   and to the prophets, "Do not prophesy to us what is right;
speak to us smooth things,
>   prophesy illusions,
leave the way, turn aside from the path,
>   let us hear no more of the Holy One of Israel.
>   (Isa. 30:10-11)

I refer again to what Neil Postman said: We have congregations that expect their wishes and wants to be met but become upset when the message of the pastor and lay leaders addresses their needs and not their wants and wishes.

Deeper Needs of the Star Performer

When I look at star performers, I see needs beyond their penchant for excitement, stimulation, and freedom from boredom. I see these needs, which the church can address:

A need for friendship that is steadfast and durable. Friendship that does not hand them back and forth to others, as was the case in their early years. They need a relationship to God, as described in Psalm 100:5:

> For the Lord is good;
> >   his steadfast love endures forever
> >   and his faithfulness to all generations.

These people may tire of you and race on to new, exciting people. They may decide to go to another church, but you can interpret what is happening and tell them that they deserve something more lasting, responsible, and faithful. One sign of maturity is to form and maintain lasting, durable relationships. You and your church can offer this durability. You can stay by these people through thick and thin, in times of great celebration and severe grief and loneliness. You will not forsake them when they run out of opportunities for excitement, stimulation, and freedom from boredom.

Often star performers are essentially lonely people. Their shallow and short-lived friendships do not really satisfy their loneliness. A group centered on spirituality, mentioned below, can speak to this loneliness. Sometimes friendships run amok because star performers are not aware of their personal boundaries. Yet group members can stabilize these boundaries and make the friendship more secure and beneficial.

I also see a need for a richer spiritual life. If your church has a group dedicated to deepening the spiritual life (and if this group has a wise and considerate leader), a star performer could profit by attending this group. This provides the opportunity to move beyond the superficial and shallow spirituality characteristic of the star performer's life. If you do not have such a group, you and this star performer can collaborate in sponsoring one. This speaks to the star performer's need to be in the limelight as it gives her an opportunity to face up to the shallowness of her spiritual life.

Probably the most profound way of caring for star performers is by gently confronting them about their main purpose or calling in life. You might ask if they have ever thought of studying drama or participating in amateur drama groups in the community. You might affirm their gifts as performers and encourage them to bring it under discipline and development. God has a place in God's creation for all who follow the gleam of God's calling.

Conclusion

The troublesomeness of people, as I have said before, may well be "runaway creativity" that needs to be slowed down to a contemplative pace. It may be the stuff of God's calling that plainly needs direction, purpose, and appropriate expression. Our calling in caring for troublesome people is to search out their gifts with them and challenge them to the consecration of their gifts to God and in considerate use of them in relation to God's community of faith.

To come to this point with troublesome people represents no small demand on us as pastors and lay leaders. But my life—and I'm sure yours —has been enriched by troublesome people. The church throughout history has dramatized the depths of the gospel. The appeal here is that the depth and seriousness of the good news of Jesus Christ be dramatized, not trivialized. The key is to help people cross the gulf between undisciplined and disciplined drama.

We have come to a stopping place in our quest for ways to care for troublesome people—the backbiter, the authoritarian person, the competitive person, the dependent person, and the star performer. I know I have not covered all types of troublesome parishioners. There's the eccentric, the chronically suicidal, the sexually promiscuous person who acts out in the congregation. . . . If you identify other kinds of troublesome people, please let me know.[1]

In discussing the five prototypes, I have given some clues and principles for a strategy for caring for troublesome people. They are not inflexible rules. They are guidelines summarized here:

First, our own personal self-examination is a form of spiritual housekeeping discipline. A pastoral support group can be a sustaining grace. There you and your colleagues can be frank about irritations with troublesome people. You can celebrate some of your wise and creative people. Fresh hope appears as you share with and pray for one another. I have such a group that meets every Tuesday at 7:30 in the morning. Such a group cannot remove the responsibility for individual self-searching, but it can offset the isolation and loneliness that comes with the territory of being a pastor or lay leader.

Second, an effort has been made in this book to emphasize the *care of*—rather than manipulation or isolation of—the troublesome person. With reason—repetition is one of the ways of ingraining a pattern or idea in our thoughts and actions—I've reiterated the importance of face-to-face relationships between people who are at odds with each other. I have based this principle on the teachings of Jesus and Paul. Jesus calls us to take quick initiative toward people who have something against us; we are to get right with them (Matt. 5:23-24). In Matthew 18:15-20

Jesus outlines a pattern of persuasion with which to seek our offender's attention, "ear," and reconciliation. The objective is to gain the confidence and respect of the one who has offended us. The apostle Paul in Galatians 6:1-2, 5 admonishes us to restore an offender in a spirit of gentleness without heavy-handedness.

I have found that this principle of face-to-face caring for troublesome people works when we are on a level ground with each other. In the case of an employee initiating such reconciliation with a supervisor, one must be courageous indeed and be ready to seek other employment if the approach were to lead to dismissal. This potential for penalization or dismissal causes many pastors to say that Jesus' and Paul's teachings won't work today. They will work if we have the courage and the ability to take the risk.

Third, I've suggested that one care for the troublesome person by seeing and relating to him in the context of the *system* of the church and community. The person is not to be isolated and treated as a scapegoat. She is a part of the larger whole. The church becomes a stifling community when it is a closed system or a living, vital community when it is an open system. A troublesome person is sometimes punished or expelled, when in fact her troublesomeness may be a symptom of a closed system with an authoritarian leader.[2]

Fourth, I have emphasized the seriousness and depth of the life, work, crucifixion, and resurrection of Jesus the Christ in contrast to the entertainment shows of television and megachurches. This shallow motif of worship has infiltrated many smaller churches. Soren Kierkegaard calls their leaders "apostles of empty enthusiasm." It reflects the general cultural process of "amusing ourselves to death," as described by the title of a book by Neil Postman.[3] This issue calls for an agonizing appraisal of the driving commitments of churches, pastors, leadership, and smaller organizations of the church. I advise using Postman's brief book as a study guide for a retreat of the official board of the church.

By no means am I suggesting that we sacrifice genuine spiritual joy and spontaneity in the life of the church. I am confident that the depths of the gospel can be expressed with joy, thanksgiving, and genuine humor. The problem with the entertainment motif is its superficiality and shallowness.

Actually, this book itself, if you have persevered with me, could be considered a "downer"—concentrating on troublesome people. I hope not! Some of the antics of the troublesome people I have mentioned can be downright funny. In caring for them we must get them to laugh with us and assure them that we are taking them seriously. Especially with the dependent person, we might ask, "When was the last time you had a good laugh?" In fact, that is a good question to ask ourselves. Life can get so serious that suddenly things become ridiculous! Laughter that is not filled with scorn is a balm for the troubled spirit.

This is the note on which I want to leave you, assuming we have not already parted; if you have stayed with me to this last page, I leave you with a Latin farewell: *Sursum Corda!* "Lift up your hearts!"

Introduction

1. E. James Anthony and Bertran J. Cohler, eds., *The Invulnerable Child* (New York: Guilford Press, 1987), 14.

Chapter 1

1. Soren Kierkegaard, *For Self-Examination* (Minneapolis: Augsburg, 1940), 35ff.

2. Edmund Husserl, *Ideas* (New York: Collier Books, 1962), 98.

3. T. B. Maston, *Biblical Ethics: A Guide to the Ethical Message of the Scriptures* (Macon, Ga.: Mercer University Press, 1991).

Chapter 2

1. Karen Horney, *Our Inner Conflicts* (New York: W. W. Norton, 1965), 40-41.

2. Gordon Allport, *The Psychology of Rumor* (New York: Henry Holt, 1947).

3. "Clinton Meets Religious Leaders," *Christian Century*, 6 October 1993, 931.

4. The following books will be very helpful: Speed B. Leas, *Leadership and Conflict* (Nashville: Abingdon Press, 1982); Speed B. Leas, *Moving Your Church through Conflict* (Bethesda, Md.: The Alban Institute, 1985); Larry L. McSwain and William C. Treadmill, *Conflict Ministry in the Church* (Nashville: Broadman Press, 1981).

5. Contact the consulting department at The Alban Institute, 4550 Montgomery Ave., Suite 433 North, Bethesda, MD 20814-3341.

6. Two books are especially helpful and provide guidelines for confronting and caring for sex offenders. See Marie M. Fortune, *Is Nothing Sacred?* (San Francisco: Harper & Row, 1989); G. Lloyd Rediger, *Ministry and Sexuality: Cases, Care, and Counseling* (Minneapolis: Fortress Press, 1990).

7. See *Christian Century*, 30 June 1993, 667.

Chapter 3

1. Michael and Deboarah Bradshaw Jinkins, *Power and Change in Parish Ministry* (Bethesda, Md.: The Alban Institute, 1991) 11.

2. John C. Harris, *Stress, Power, and Ministry* (Bethesda, Md.: The Alban Institute, 1977), 69.

3. E. P. Hollander, *Leaders, Groups, and Influence* (New York: Oxford Press, 1964), 167-69.

4. Harris, *Stress, Power, and Ministry*, 78.

5. T. W. Adorno, et al., *The Authoritarian Personality* (New York: Harper & Row, 1950).

6. Friedrich Nietzsche, *The Joyful Wisdom*, trans. Thomas Common (N.Y.: Frederick Ungar, 1960), par. 168.

Chapter 4

1. Robert Bellah, et al., *Habits of the Heart: Individualism and Commitment in American Life* (Berkeley: University of California Press, 1985), 55-103.

Chapter 5

1. Erik Erikson, *Identity and the Life Cycles* (New York: International University Press, 1960), 65.

2. Carl Rogers, *Client-Centered Therapy* (New York: Houghton Mifflin, 1951), 41.

3. Stanley W. Jackson, M.D., "The Listening Healer in the History of Psychological Healing," *American Journal of Psychiatry* 149, no. 12 (December 1992): 1629.

4. "Looking at the World Upside Down: An Interview with Robert Coles," *Christian Century*, 1 December 1993, 1210.

Chapter 6

1. Wayne E. Oates, *Behind the Masks: Personality Disorders in Religious Behaviors* (Louisville: Westminster Press, 1987), 32-42.

2. *As You Like It*, act 2, sc. 4, lines 130-139.

3. Theodore Millon, *Disorders of Personality DSM III* (New York: John Wiley, 1981), 152, 155.

4. Soren Kierkegaard, *Either/Or*, vol. 1, trans. David and Lillian Marian Swenson (Princeton, N.J.: Princeton University Press, 1949), 231.

5. Neil Postman, *Amusing Ourselves to Death: Public Discourse in the Age of Show* (New York: Penguin Books, 1986). 116-117.

6. G. Lloyd Rediger, *Ministry and Sexuality: Cases, Care and Counseling* (Minneapolis: Fortress Press, 1990), 18-19.

Epilogue

1. I can be reached at 3500 Winchester Rd., Louisville, KY 40207.

2. For further reading on systems thinking, see Ludwig von Bertalanffy, *General Systems Theory* (New York: George Braziller, 1968); Edwin H. Friedman, *Generation to Generation: Family Process in Church and Synagogue* (New York: Guilford Press, 1985).

3. Neil Postman, *Amusing Ourselves to Death: Public Discourse in the Age of Show* (New York: Penguin Books, 1986).

The Alban Institute:
an invitation to membership

The Alban Institute, begun in 1979, believes that the congregation is essential to the task of equipping the people of God to minister in the church and the world. A multi-denominational membership organization, the Institute provides on-site training, educational programs, consulting, research, and publishing for hundreds of churches across the country.

The Alban Institute invites you to be a member of this partnership of laity, clergy, and executives—a partnership that brings together people who are raising important questions about congregational life and people who are trying new solutions, making new discoveries, finding a new way of getting clear about the task of ministry. The Institute exists to provide you with the kinds of information and resources you need to support your ministries.

Join us now and enjoy these benefits:

CONGREGATIONS, The Alban Journal, a highly respected journal published six times a year, to keep you up to date on current issues and trends.

Inside Information, Alban's quarterly newsletter, keeps you informed about research and other happenings around Alban. Available to members only.

Publications Discounts:

- ☐ 15% for Individual, Retired Clergy, and Seminarian Members
- ☐ 25% for Congregational Members
- ☐ 40% for Judicatory and Seminary Executive Members

Discounts on Training and Education Events

Write our Membership Department at the address below or call us at 1-800-486-1318 or 301-718-4407 for more information about how to join The Alban Institute's growing membership, particularly about Congregational Membership in which 12 designated persons receive all benefits of membership.

The Alban Institute, Inc.
Suite 433 North
4550 Montgomery Avenue
Bethesda, MD 20814-3341